THE MARVELS OF CREATION

Cover & interior design by www.davidferrisdesign.com

Image Credits

Cover

Third Day of Creation, Genesis, Schnorr von Carolsfeld, Julius (1794-1872) / Lebrecht Authors / Bridgeman Images

AngryBrush, Morphart Creation, Danussa, Christos Georghiou, Hein Nouwens, oleskalashnik, Channarong Pherngjanda, sar14ev, Manekina Serafima, Golden Shrimp © Shutterstock.com

Interior images

pgs 2, 123, 137: Traditional Line Art, St. Edmund Campion Missal & Hymnal for the Traditional Latin Mass © Corpus Christi Watershed

pg 13: Tatiana Apanasova and Nastasia Lagoda © Shutterstock.com

pg 20: sar14ev © Shutterstock.com

pg 29: Christos Georghiou © Shutterstock.com

pgs 40, 45, 77: Channarong Pherngjanda © Shutterstock.com

pgs 46, 58, 83, 87, 94, 102, 107: Hein Nouwens © Shutterstock.com

pgs 53, 58, 64, 87, 105, 144: Morphart Creation © Shutterstock.com

pgs 80: AVA Bitter © Shutterstock.com

pg 149: Third Day of Creation, Genesis, Schnorr von Carolsfeld, Julius (1794-1872) / Lebrecht Authors / Bridgeman Images

ISBN: 9781505114812

Library of Congress Control Number: 2019950690

Published in the United States by

TAN Books
PO Box 410487
Charlotte, NC 28241
www.TANBooks.com

Printed in the United States of America 2019

THE MARVELS OF CREATION

Ven. Luis of Granada, OP

Edited and arranged by
Ryan Grant

TAN Books
Charlotte, North Carolina

TABLE OF CONTENTS

EDITOR'S NOTE

The Venerable Louis of Granada was a 16th century Spanish Dominican. He is celebrated as a theologian of great merit, and the author of numerous spiritual works, such as the *Sinner's Guide*.

In this holy Dominican's meditation on creation, you will find no polemical work of any sort. In our day debates about creation and questions raised by modern science cause a great deal of contention and consternation. However, in the *Marvels of Creation*, these debates are far from the mind of the author. This is not merely because the work was written four centuries ago, but even more so, because his aim is one specific thing: that man might see the wonders that God has put in plain sight and give glory to Him for them. Thus, the reader can take the book in confidence and find herein great spiritual fruit, whatever his views are in relation to modern questions on creation.

Nevertheless, though the author writes as a theologian and only means to present the science as it was in his own day, just the same, discoveries subsequent to his time have allowed for the formulation of new principles and led to the rejection of older ideas in favor of more precise modern formulations. So, when the author makes reference to Aristotle's notion of the four elements, or Galen's teaching of the humors, these theories of ancient learning are best looked upon as superseded rather than merely wrong. The theory of the humors, for what it was meant to explain, is not wrong per se, but it is too broad to be precise, let alone isolate phenomena or predict events based on principles. Likewise, the theory of the four elements, which is not wrong in observing that some things go down and others tend to go up, is still wrong as to the causes of such things. In both areas, modern science affords us more precise theories that more accurately describe what takes place and allow us to predict other events based on them. Whenever it is advantageous to the reader, we have placed footnotes where a claim or comparison by the author has been superseded or corrected by modern scientific knowledge.

None of this should trouble the reader when he comes across an antiquated description of events. In fact, noting our more precise scientific theories in physics or cosmology, we should give God glory all the more for the complicated workings of the created world that we find all around us, and of which we are, nevertheless, the pinnacle.

Therefore, let the reader carefully and prayerfully consider the wisdom of Fr. Granada, and look with wonder at all things, great and small, which our creator God has placed in the world for us.

–The Editor

AUTHOR'S INTRODUCTION

In the following work, our aim is none other than that man should glorify Almighty God by seeing His providence and care at work in creation. We shall look at the works of the creator that are both great and small, complex and simple, to see His handiwork not only in the marvelous arrangement of stars and planets, but of tiny ants and bees which we overlook on account of their size.

To do this, I shall quote from many authors who observed these marvels while adding commentary to them so as to fix the mind of the reader inextricably on God. There is nothing in this work that will not seem positively wondrous and which will not give further testimony of the wisdom and providence of God who made all these things.

The interpretation and application of these marvels I leave to the devotion and prudence of the reader. If I were to comment on each detail, the discussion would be too lengthy. I should like only to remind the reader that man is created in the image and likeness of God because of his immortal soul, which is illumined with the light of reason. As a result, man is not only able to know divine things, but also to establish and govern nations, with all their necessary offices and functions. But the reader should realize that while man does all these things through the light of reason with which he has been endowed, God's smallest creatures perform many of the same functions much better than does man himself, although they lack the use of reason. Moreover, while man can indeed devise many marvels, whether they be great buildings or great works of the mind, the great creations of God that light the heavens, and the mighty animals of the earth eclipse his endeavors.

This applies to many of the things we shall now describe, and we should remember that God did all this to manifest His greatness and providence, so that knowing these things, we would honor and reverence Him.

–The Ven. Louis of Granada

1

CREATION OF THE WORLD

Sacred scripture tells us of the immensity and greatness of our Creator. This fact of revelation may also be understood by making a simple exploration into the world He created, since it gives clear testimony to God's greatness.

One of the many differences between the Creator and His creatures is that all created things have limits and boundaries to which their natures and powers extend. As a result, they have a limited or finite being and limited powers, knowledge, and faculties that flow from that being. This limitation is according to the measure that the Creator willed to impart to His creatures, giving more to some and less to others.

Seeing that God Himself was not created by any superior being, there is no being that can put limits or

boundaries to His essence, power, knowledge, goodness, happiness, or any of His other perfections and attributes. Now, since there are no limits or restrictions of any kind in God, He is infinite in every respect. Therefore, His being is infinite, as are all of His other attributes, such as His beauty, His glory, His richness, His mercy, and His justice. Because He is incomprehensible and ineffable, no creature that has been made or could be made will ever comprehend Him. God alone can perfectly know and comprehend Himself.

Comparing the relationship between the Creator and His creatures with that of a king and his subordinates, we can readily grasp the notion of God's infinity. They distribute the duties and offices in their kingdom at their pleasure to various persons, limiting the jurisdiction and power given to each one lest it be prejudicial to others. The king who thus restricts this delegated power, possesses in himself the supreme and universal authority throughout his entire kingdom, so that he acknowledges no one superior to himself. As a result, there is in the kingdom no jurisdiction or power, however great, that the king does not surpass. We call such jurisdiction and power infinite or absolute, in the sense that it is not restricted to any limit or boundary within its own area of jurisdiction.

We can demonstrate the same truth in another way. According to philosophers and theologians, God is so great a being that it is impossible that a being greater than He exists. One could not even imagine a greater or more perfect being than God. If the perfections of God were in any way limited, we would be able to imagine other perfections greater than His. But this is impossible, for we have already stated that our concept of God is that of a being so great that we could not even imagine one that is greater.

Let us take as our theme the words of the angel who represented the person of God. When the father of Samson asked his name he replied: "Why do you ask my name, which is wonderful?"(Judg. 13:18) This is a word well suited to the greatness of God and all His works, for there is nothing however small which, if well considered, will not cause hearts to marvel at the Creator, saying to us in His name: "Why do you ask my name, which is wonderful?"

God created all things out of love of Himself, that is to say, as a manifestation of the greatness of His perfections. If a man is not filled with admiration and wonder when he contemplates the works of the Creator, it is because he does not understand them. Their majesty and brilliance are sufficient to utterly dazzle the human mind. But our intellects cannot easily encompass so immense a world and all the things that are in it. Rather, we would be overwhelmed if we tried to consider all these marvelous things at the same time.

Creation, in its proper sense, does not mean to make one thing from another (this is called generation), but to make something from nothing. Such a power is proper to God, and it cannot be communicated to any creature, however perfect. Observing the changes that take place in natural things, we see that the greater the distance from one extreme to the other, the greater the power required to cause such a change. Still, the distance between non-being and being is infinite. So, an infinite power is required for the work of creation. This power is found in God alone, who "calls those things that are not, as those that are" (Romans 4:17).

As we delve into the marvels of creation, we shall first

treat of the world, the heavens and the elements. Then we shall treat in particular of all living bodies, such as plants, animals, and finally man. My intention is not merely to declare that there is a God who is Creator and Lord of all things. Rather, I endeavor to demonstrate the divine providence that shines forth in all creatures, as well as the three other perfections that accompany it, especially the divine goodness, wisdom, and omnipotence, for these are, as Isaiah says, the three fingers on which God has poised the bulk of the earth (Isaiah 40:12).

These three perfections are all one in God, but each has its own purpose. Divine goodness desires to bring benefits to His creatures, divine wisdom plans and ordains how this is to be done, and divine omnipotence executes and effects what His goodness desires and His wisdom ordains. These three perfections are, so to speak, the constituent parts of divine providence whereby God, with a pious and fatherly concern, furnishes a wide variety of things that His creatures need. These three divine perfections and countless others shine forth in all the things of this world, the great as well as the small.

The words of David show us how wonderful the study of the divine perfections really is: "Blessed are they that search His testimonies; that seek Him with their whole heart" (Psalm 118 [119]:2). And they will be no less blessed who search God's works; not only those of grace, but also those of nature, because they all spring from the same source. Uncreated Wisdom promises: "They that explain Me shall have life everlasting" (Sirach 24:31). That is what we are seeking to do here: to reveal the plan of divine Wisdom as it is manifested in all created things.

A great aid in acquiring rhetorical skill is to observe the plan and technique that a great orator employs in his speeches. St. Augustine considered it extremely helpful that he himself had done so in regard to certain passages in St. Paul (*Christian Doctrine*, 4). How much better a study it is to observe the admirable plan of divine wisdom in the structure and government of the created universe. And if it is written of the Queen of Saba that "she had no longer any spirit in her" (3 [1] Kings 10:5), when she saw all the wisdom of Solomon and the house that he had built, how much more will the devout soul be humbled when, gazing upon the works of incomprehensible wisdom, he seeks to understand the means and prudence that made them?

2

THE SPLENDOR OF THE SKY

The divine perfections are reflected in the created works of God so that our hearts may be moved to love the goodness of God, and our minds aroused to a holy awe and reverence for such great majesty. Let us also be inspired with hope in His paternal care and providence and with greater admiration for the mighty power and wisdom that shine forth through the works of His hands.

We accept as a fundamental proposition that the most gracious and sovereign Lord determined to create man and place him in this world through His infinite goodness. By knowing, loving, and obeying his Creator man might merit the happiness of the world to come. He also determined to provide man with all the things necessary for his sustenance and preservation. Consequently, God created the visible world and all things in it for the use and necessities of human life.

In any workshop two things are required: the material from which things are made and the worker who makes the things. In the great workshop of the universe, these two requirements have been amply provided for by the Creator. The material from which new things are made is the variety of elements, and the agents that generate new things from the elements are the heavenly bodies, such as the planets and stars. While God is the First Cause and moves every other cause, these heavenly bodies are among the principal instruments that God uses for the government of the world.

Since the heavenly bodies are among the principal agents of the First Mover, God has ennobled them and made them excel over all other bodies. They are seemingly incorruptible, so that even after so many ages since they were created, they appear to continue in the same perfection and beauty that they possessed from the beginning. Time, the destroyer of all things, seems not to have impaired any of them.[1]

God also endowed them with brilliant light, both to adorn the universe, and to benefit human life. The Psalmist declares: "Praise ye the Lord of lords . . . who made the great lights, . . . the sun to rule the day . . . the moon and the stars

[1] Editor's note: In the sixteenth century, the phases of stars, supernovas, etc. were still unknown. Nevertheless, this weakness in the astronomy of his day does not mitigate the general thrust of de Granada's argument. Generation to generation the stars and other heavenly bodies appear to us the same.

to rule the night" (Psalm 135 [136]:3-9). He gave them such constancy in their movements that they never seem to have varied from the orderly motion that He placed in them from the beginning. As a result, all those whose function it is to rule and govern others, either in the Church or in nations, can learn from the planets how well regulated and constant they must be in their lives to prevent disorder in the lives of those under their care. If the light that is supposed to illumine the darkness went out, then how great the darkness will be! And if one blind man leads another, what is to be expected but that both will fall?

The heavenly bodies are so magnificent that they cause admiration in anyone who considers them. And the beauty of the sky, who can describe it? How pleasant it is, in the serenity of a midsummer's night, to see the full moon in all its brightness, surpassing in clarity the light of all the stars! And when there is no moon, what is more enchanting and more indicative of the omnipotence and beauty of God than the vast heavens sprinkled with a variety of stars, so numerous that no one can count them except He that made them? But habitually seeing these things so often robs us of admiration for their beauty and of the incentive to praise the divine Artist who has thus beautified the mighty vault of the heavens.

Let us suppose there was a child that was born in a prison and lived there until he reached the age of manhood, without ever seeing anything outside the prison walls. Now, if he had become a man of intelligence and learning, then the first time he left the prison and saw the starry sky on a tranquil night, he could not help but be astonished at such great beauty. Nor could he do anything else but say: "Who could have adorned the heavens with so many precious jewels and with diamonds so brilliant? Who could have created such a great number of lamps to give light to the world? Who could have filled the meadow of the skies with such a variety of flowers? Who, but some most beautiful and omnipotent Creator?"

A classical philosopher once said: "To look at the heavens is to become a philosopher." In other words, when one contemplates the great variety and beauty of the sky, he recognizes the wisdom and power of its Author. The Psalmist speaks in the same way: "O Lord our Lord, how admirable is Your name in the whole earth! For Your magnificence is elevated above the heavens.... For I will behold Your heavens, the works of Your fingers; the moon and the stars which You have founded" (Psalm 8:2–4).

If the beauty of the planets is admirable, no less remarkable is the influence they exert on the things of the earth. This is especially true of the sun. For example, when it is farthest removed from the earth,[2] as during the autumn and winter, the trees and bushes lose their foliage and become sterile and almost dead. Then in the spring, when it is closer to the earth, the fields are again dressed in green, the trees are covered with buds and leaves, and the vines and bushes bring forth new shoots, as if impatient

[2] Editor's note: This was the prevailing view in the 16th century, but today we know that the colder seasons are not caused by distance but rather the earth's tilt away from the sun in those seasons, and likewise its tilt toward the sun in warmer seasons.

to manifest the beauty that they contain hidden within themselves. So many marvelous qualities are to be found in the sun that when the ancient philosopher Anaxagoras was asked why he was born, he answered that it was to see the sun.

But although the sun is so remarkable a body, few persons marvel at the powers and virtues which the Creator has given it, because the habit of seeing things that always do the same thing causes them to become plain and ordinary. No one marvels at things as long as they follow their routine, but when they depart from it, everyone is amazed and wonders what the change means. Men marvel at new things rather than at great things. However, St. Augustine says, wise men marvel more at great things than at new and unusual things, because they have eyes to see the dignity and excellence of the former and to evaluate them properly.

One of the greatest and most universal effects of the sun is that it gives light and brilliance to all the other planets and stars that are scattered throughout the sky. And since these lesser planets exert their influence on the world by means of the light that they receive from the sun, it follows that, after God, the sun is the first cause of all generation, corruption, change, and alteration which takes place in the world. The sun also draws the vapors of the oceans on high and when they reach the regions where the air is very cool, they condense and are turned into rain which irrigates the land, thus producing the fruits and grains that nourish animals and men. In this sense we can say that the sun gives us bread, wine, meat, fruits, and nearly everything else that is necessary for life.

It is also the sun that causes the four seasons of the year, as its distance from the earth is lessened and increased. Divine providence regulates these seasons both for the health of our bodies and for the production of the fruits of the earth by which we are sustained, and so equally is the time divided among them that none of them prevails over the other. By means of the four seasons, the divine Ruler sustains and governs this world, increasing His family each year and providing food and nourishment for it. Who, then, seeing the order of divine providence, would not cry out with the Psalmist: "How great are Your works, O Lord; You have made all things in wisdom; the earth is filled with Your riches" (Psalm 103 [104]:24)?

By its presence or absence, the sun also divides time into day and night, to the happiness and welfare of the earth's inhabitants. The day is of greater benefit to the needs of human life, while the night is more beneficial to the plants of the earth, for after the long warm days, plants are refreshed by the coolness and dew of the night hours, whereas at night men and animals, fatigued with the labors of the day, take their rest. The night is also the most suitable time for man to refresh his soul with spiritual things, for then he is freed from the cares and business of the day. Then he can meditate in silence on the goodness of God, singing His praises, as David says: "In the daytime the Lord hath commanded His mercy, and a canticle to Him in the night. With me is prayer to the God of my life. I will say

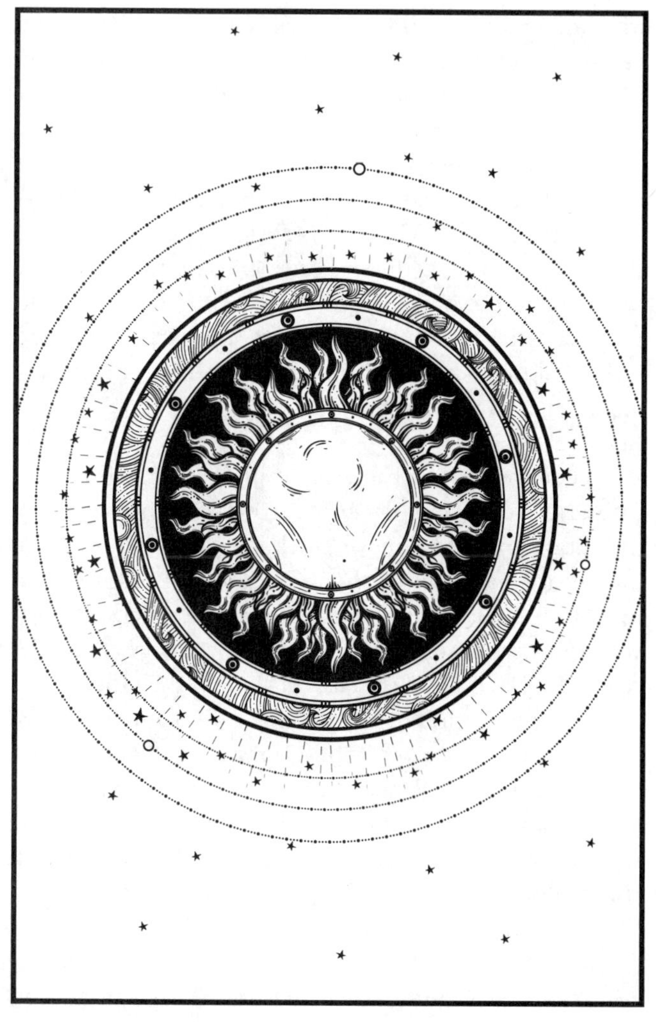

to God: You are my support" (Psalm 41 [42]:9-10). To this practice of prayer David especially invites those who live in the house of the Lord, saying: "Behold, now bless ye the Lord, all ye servants of the Lord who stand in the house of the Lord, in the courts of the house of our God. In the night lift up your hands to the holy places, and bless ye the Lord" (Psalm 133 [134]:1-2). Jeremiah calls men to the same duty with these words: "Rise up at midnight, and pour forth your heart as water before God," and the prophet Isaiah lifted up his soul to God and exclaimed: "My soul longed for You in the night; and in the morning early with my spirit within me I will watch for You" (Isaiah 26:9).

Therefore, in the calm, silent night, bring your heart to humble devotion, fixing your eyes on the beauty of the moon or the splendor of the stars which proclaim the beauty and glory of their Creator. The brightness of the stars foretells the beauty of the glorified bodies which will be ours on the day of resurrection. "There are bodies celestial, and bodies terrestrial, but one is the glory of the celestial and another of the terrestrial. One is the glory of the sun, another the glory of the moon, and another the glory of the stars, for star differs from star in glory. So also, is the resurrection of the dead. It is sown in corruption; it shall rise in incorruption. It is sown in dishonor; it shall rise in glory. It is sown in weakness; it shall rise in power" (1 Corinthians 15:40-43).

In addition to all these things, the sun so enlightens everything that God has created in the heavens and on the earth, that nothing is hidden from it. And as the sun is the most visible of all corporeal things and the one least able to be gazed upon because of its great brilliance and the weakness of our vision, so also God is the most intelligible of all beings. Yet, He is the one least comprehended because of the magnificence of His essence and the lowliness of our understanding. Likewise, of all bodily creatures, the sun is the most communicative of light and heat, so that if one closes the door to keep out the sun, it enters through the chinks of the door. What better symbol of the infinite goodness of God, who communicates His riches so abundantly to all creatures!

From the resplendent brilliance of the sun the stars receive their brightness and efficacy. In this same way, just as from the plenitude and abundance of the grace of Christ, the Savior, all just souls receive light and power to perform good works. Moreover, as the presence of the sun is the cause of light and its absence results in darkness, so also the presence of Christ in souls enlightens and teaches them, shows them the way to heaven, and points out the obstacles that must be avoided. But when He is absent from souls, they remain in darkness and obscurity. Thus, they stumble and fall into a thousand occasions of sin, without knowing what they do or realizing what a great danger it is to their salvation when they so live.

The sun manifests the perfections of God in so many ways. What more delightful and beautiful sight could there be than that of the sun when it rises in the morning? With the clarity of its splendor it dispels the darkness and sheds its light on all things, bringing joy to the heavens, the earth, and the sea. We can compare its beauty to that of a bridegroom and its strength to that of a giant.

Now, the Creator has committed to the moon the task of providing light in the absence of the sun, otherwise the world would be left in total darkness. In addition to many other characteristics, the moon has great power over the waters of the ocean. As the magnet draws iron filings to itself, so the Creator gave to the moon the power of attracting to itself the waters of the ocean, thus causing the ebb and flow of the tides. The moon holds the reins, so to speak, whereby it controls the ocean.

In addition to its power over the ocean, the moon also influences the bodies of men and animals. Thus, we notice that when the moon is full or in its crescent phase, there are greater or lesser changes in the human body, especially in the sick. There is a remarkable power that the Creator has given to this moon, in spite of the fact that it is so distant from the earth and has no light of itself, but receives it from the sun.

Lastly, who but the Lord can describe the number, power, and effects of the stars? The Psalmist (Psalm 146:4), reveals the complete dependence of the stars on their Creator, who caused the things which do not exist to come into being, giving existence to those things that do not have it (Romans 4:17).

Of this dependence and obedience, the prophet Baruch says: "And the stars have given light in their watches, and rejoiced. They were called, and they said:

Here we are. And with cheerfulness they have shined forth to Him that made them" (Baruch 3:34-35). In saying that God calls each one by name, the prophet means that He alone knows the properties and nature of the stars and that He has given them their names accordingly. No human tongue can speak of these things, for they are reserved to divine wisdom. Among the many uses and benefits of the stars is to serve as guides for those who sail the seas. Since there are no markings in the waters by which the sailor can direct his navigation, he raises his eyes to the heavens and finds his guidance in the stars, especially in the North Star, which never changes but serves as a stable and certain guide.

3

BENEFITS OF AIR AND RAIN

In treating of each of the elements let us begin by considering the numerous benefits of the air. Men and animals are able to breathe because of the air. The coolness of the air refreshes them and cools the heat of their bodies. It is also the medium through which the light of the sun reaches them, at the same time that it diffuses the light rays so that the heat of the sun is beneficial rather than harmful.

The air also performs an important function in the production of rain. The heat of the sun causes vapors to rise from the waters of the earth and when these vapors reach the upper regions where the air is cold, they condense into drops of water and fall from the skies as rain. We witness a similar phenomenon in distilleries or perfumeries, where the intense heat of the fire drives the moisture from the herbs or flowers and the vapor ascends to a cooler area, condenses into liquid, and then drips into the vessel prepared for it. This is another example of how art imitates nature.

It is likewise a cause of admiration to see how the Creator has ordained that the rains should fall from above. If all the wise men of the world were to discuss in what way the earth should be irrigated, they could not find a more convenient and effective method than this one. The water falls from the heavens as if it were run through the small holes of a sieve, and is equally distributed over all parts of the ground. It penetrates into the earth itself to give nourishment to plants at their roots, while externally it refreshes the leaves and fruits of the trees.

This is one of God's marvels to which Job refers when he says: "He binds up the waters in His clouds, so that they do not break out and fall down together" (Job 26:8). Moses also writes in praise of the Promised Land: "For the land which you go to possess is not like the land of Egypt, from where you came out, where, when the seed is sown, waters are brought in to water it, after the manner of gardens. But it is a land of hills and plains, expecting rain from heaven. And the Lord your God always visits it, and His eyes are on it from the beginning of the year unto its end. If then you obey my commandments, which I command you this day, that you love the Lord your God, and serve Him with all your heart, and with all your soul, He will give to your land the early rain and the latter rain, that you may gather in your corn, and your wine, and your oil,

and your hay out of the fields to feed your cattle, and that you may eat and be filled" (Deuteronomy 11:10–15). The Psalmist likewise sings the praise of this blessing when he says: "Who covers the heaven with clouds, and prepares rain for the earth" (Psalm 146:8). Again, Job says that God not only irrigates the seeded and tilled lands but even the deserted places and the uncharted paths, so that they produce green and fresh foliage.

But who could ever explain the many blessings that

come to us because of rain, let alone sufficiently praise them? It is because of the rain that we have bread, wine, oil, fruits, vegetables, medicinal herbs, and pasture for the animals that provide our meat as well as the wool and leather for our clothing and shoes. The Psalmist was aware of this when he said that God "makes grass to grow on the mountains, and herbs for the service of men" (Psalm 146:8). He also states that man gives food to animals because the animals, in turn, do much for man. So numerous are the benefits that we receive from the rain that one of the ancient Greek philosophers maintained that water is the material from which all things are made.

The blessings of rain are truly great and universal! Yet, the Creator Himself holds the keys to it and reserves to Himself its distribution. He uses it to give sustenance to His faithful and chastisement to the rebellious, by depriving them of this benefit. So it is written in the book of Job that God judges and punishes His people in this way (Job 36:31), and in the Book of Leviticus we read how God will provide for His faithful ones: "If you walk in My precepts, and keep My commandments, and do them, I will give you rain in due season. And the ground shall bring forth its increase, and the trees shall be filled with fruit" (Leviticus 26:3-4). But for those who despise His laws and condemn His judgments, God promises that He will visit them with poverty and a burning heat that will destroy their lives. They shall sow their seed in vain, and the ground will not bring forth its increase nor the trees yield their fruit (Leviticus 26:14).

It is not only for sin, but also ingratitude for such great blessings that can cause us to lose them, as we learn through the words of Jeremiah: "They have not said in their heart: Let us fear the Lord our God, who gives us the early and the latter rain in due season; who preserves for us the fullness of the yearly harvest" (Jeremiah 5:24). Surely it is a great cause of sorrow that there are so few who acknowledge this great blessing from the Creator, especially since He gives us so many other things through the bountiful rain that we could not subsist without it. We should think of these things when we see the rain falling from the heavens. Otherwise we imitate the irrational animals, who receive pasture and sustenance from God but neither acknowledge the Giver nor give thanks to Him because they lack reason.

The wind is another blessing from divine providence and the Psalmist acknowledged it as such when he stated: "He brings forth winds out of His treasury" (Psalm 134 [135]:7). First of all, the winds carry the clouds and the waters that are in them wherever the Creator wishes those rains to be sent (Job 37:6). So, we see that it rains in Spain when the wind is from the southwest, coming in from the sea and bringing the rain clouds from that direction. On the other hand, in Africa the rains come with the north wind, which likewise passes over the sea and brings that continent the rain-filled clouds which are the water buckets of God.

Now, what would happen to navigation and ocean commerce between islands and nations if there were no winds and the air were always calm? The winds enable the navigators to travel to the very ends of the earth, so that they can collect the products that are plentiful in one place but scarce in another and bring back the things that others have in abundance but which we lack. Thus, all things are made common and all nations receive a sufficiency, and the whole world becomes a common market place. What is more, these same winds have carried the missionaries to all parts of the world and the gospel message that they brought is the better than any kind of merchandise.

The winds also serve another purpose, namely, they purify the air and remove from it any harmful substance with which it may be contaminated. All we need to do is recall the great pestilence in the city of Lisbon in 1570, which was ended when an unusually cold and strong wind carried away the germ-laden air and caused the sea water to overflow into the wells and fountains along the coastline.

The winds also help the farmer to fan the wheat and to remove dust and straw from the grain. And when he is oppressed by the withering heat of summer, a fresh breeze lessens the force of the heat and refreshes him. From these examples Christian souls can learn how to refer all things to God and how to be edified by God's works. Let them also consider how great must be the torment of the eternal flames where the damned are burning in the never-ending fire and can never hope for any sort of refreshment.

4

THE GRANDEUR OF THE SEA

We now come to the second element, water, which at the beginning of creation covered the entire earth, as the air covered all the water (Genesis 1:2). But since no one could have inhabited the earth under such conditions, the Creator, who made the earth for the service of man, just as He made man for Himself, commanded that the waters be gathered together to form seas and oceans and thus uncover the earth as our dwelling place.

There are many aspects of the oceans that are worthy of consideration, such as their grandeur, fruitfulness, and depths, their shores and ports, their risings and fallings, and, finally, the great benefits that they bring us. All these qualities preach a silent sermon of praise to Him who created them. This is why the Psalmist praised God for the grandeur of the oceans when he said: "How great are Your works, O Lord! You have made all things in wisdom; the earth is filled with Your riches. So is this great sea, which stretches its arms wide" (Psalm 103 [104]:24-25).

The Creator ordained these things for all nations to enjoy the benefits of the various bodies of water which serve to bring nations closer together by means of navigation and serve also as a source of nourishment for men by supplying a great variety of fish and other sea food. Consequently, the Creator willed that the ocean should have many bays and gulfs for fish to seek shelter so that men might catch them with greater ease. Moreover, in all the seas and oceans there are ports and harbors where ships can rest secure from storms and the violence of the winds.

The omnipotence and providence of the Creator are similarly manifested in the multitude of islands that are distributed throughout the oceans and seas. St. Ambrose compares them to little jewels that adorn the great bodies of water. God in His providence has fashioned them as a stopping-place where sailors can renew their strength, find refreshment, and take refuge in time of storm. The omnipotence of God shines forth in the conservation of these little islands, especially when the towering waves would almost seem to cover them over or the angry seas would threaten to wash them away. It is a marvel of which God spoke through the mouth of Job: "Who shut up the sea with doors, when it broke forth as issuing out of the womb; when I made a cloud the garment thereof, and wrapped it in a mist as in swaddling bands? I set My bounds around it, and made it bars and doors; and I said: Hitherto you shall come, and shalt go no further, and here you shall break your swelling waves" (Job 38:8-11).

All the elements have a tendency to seek their natural positions or places and the natural place for water, as we have seen, is to cover the entire earth. But God, by His word alone, has removed it from its natural place and has gathered it together into oceans and seas. This has not changed for many thousands of years, and the waters have not surpassed the limits that He assigned them. God uses this obedience of insensible creation as an argument to put to shame the disobedience and irreverence of men. He says through Jeremiah: "Will not you then fear Me . . . and will you not repent at My presence? I have set the sand a bound for the sea, an everlasting ordinance, which it shall not pass over; and the waves thereof shall toss themselves, and shall not prevail; they shall swell, and shall not pass over it" (Jeremiah 5:22).

Who would not be moved to adore the omnipotence and providence of the Creator who is able to establish and maintain what He wishes? He has placed a limitation and restraint on the waters of the world so that they will not cover the entire earth. Although the waves of the ocean beat furiously against the sand and shore, they never dare to pass beyond the assigned limits. Beating against the shores and boundaries of the earth, the waters of the ocean see the law of the Creator written there and turn back, much like a runaway horse feels the pull of the reins and bridle and stops and turns around, although he does not want to do so.

The sea both divides the lands and nations and promotes friendship and concord among those same nations. The Creator did not give each nation all that is necessary for life, because the dependence of one nation upon another prompts them to be friendly to each other. But the highways and roads that cross the continents are often difficult to travel and it is impossible to transport every kind of merchandise over the roads of the earth. Therefore, the Creator provided this new path on which ships both great and small could navigate and one ship can carry a cargo that would require the use of many beasts of burden. In this way the ocean is like a great fair, or market place, where all the nations of the world exchange goods and each receives the things necessary to itself.

We should note also that the ocean serves as a symbol of the meekness of God as well as His anger and indignation. What is more meek and tranquil than the ocean when it is calm and no winds blow, or when a soft and gentle breeze sends the rippling waves to the shore, where they break silently and return to the ocean in regular succession? This is a symbol of the meekness and gentleness of God toward the good and the just. Yet, sometimes the sea is buffeted by violent winds and lifts its terrifying waves high into the sky, and then, it reveals the dark chasms of its depth. Or sometimes it lashes with fierce strength against the sides of ships, raising them on high and suddenly dropping them with a jolt. When this happens, then the men who are at the mercy of the sea are in mortal fear and tremble for their lives. In this, we have a symbol of the divine wrath and of the magnitude of divine power that is able to stir up such tempests and appease them when He wills.

The Psalmist speaks of this when he says: "O Lord God of hosts, who is like to You? You are mighty, O Lord, and Your truth is round about You. You rule the power of the sea, and appease the motion of the waves thereof.... Yours are the heavens, and thine is the earth; the world and the fullness thereof You founded; the north and the sea You created" (Psalm 88 [89]:9-12).

What words could describe the wide variety of fish that are found in the sea? What great wisdom has fashioned them, not only in such a multitude of species, but in so many different shapes and sizes? Some are small and others are of incredible size, and between the two extremes there is infinite variety. The same God created the whale and the frog but He did not labor more in the making of one or the other.

Who can count the eggs of the shad or the codfish or any other fish? Yet each egg is capable of producing another fish as large as the one from which the egg originally came. Like a tender mother, the ocean receives these eggs and protects and nurtures them until they grow into fish. Although divine providence has created fish for the sustenance of men, still the fishermen cannot see the fish in the waters as the hunter sees the game on the land or in the air. So, God caused the number of fishes to be so

great that some could usually be caught wherever the net would be let down. The number and variety of animals and birds is almost countless, but greater still is the number of fishes in the sea.

How pleasing are the works of the Lord, and all are made with consummate wisdom. Consider, finally, the sweetness and taste of the various kinds of fish and sea foods. St. Ambrose exclaims that these delicacies were created before man himself. God treats us as His beloved children and He intends the tastiness of these foods to lead us to love and praise the Lord who provided them. But many men are so slothful and self-centered that although all the creatures of the world invite us to praise the Giver of all gifts, these men are so occupied with pampering their appetites that it never occurs to them to give thanks to God or to acknowledge that these things have been given to us without any merits on our part.

5

THE BEAUTY AND FERTILITY OF THE EARTH

The earth is our common mother, from which man's body originally came and by which we are nourished. Of all the elements, the earth is the lowest and least active, yet it does more for us than any other. The Psalmist declares: "The heaven of heaven is the Lord's, but the earth He has given to the children of men" (Psalm 113 [114]:16). In obedience to the command of God, the earth receives us as a kindly mother when we are born, sustains us after we are born, and at the end of our life again receives us into her lap, faithfully guarding our bodies until the day of resurrection.

The earth is also gentler to us than the other elements.

The oceans and rivers sometimes cause tidal waves and floods that do considerable damage to men and their property. The air is sometimes whipped into tornadoes, hurricanes, or windstorms that damage the crops and destroy the work of poor laborers. But the earth is the faithful servant of man. What fruits it produces! What beautiful colors it presents! And who could describe the riches of the earth, especially when we consider the variety of metals that were taken from it for thousands of years before the coming of Christ and have been mined since that time and will be extracted until the end of time.

Still more noteworthy are the wellsprings and rivers that irrigate and refresh the earth. As the Creator has placed veins and arteries throughout the human body to sustain and refresh it, so also, He has provided a network of rivers to refresh and irrigate the great body of the earth. But in many parts of the earth there is a deficiency of springs and rivers, and so divine providence has ordained that the whole earth should be saturated with water, so that by digging wells men can supply for the lack of springs or rivers.

Again, who will not be filled with wonder at the wellspring and mouth from which these rivers and springs flow? In many lands far removed from the sea we discover wide ribbons of water cutting across the plains or gushing springs racing down the mountain sides. What is the source of this water? How is it that the water flows at all times of the year, both in winter and summer, and never runs dry even after thousands of years? The Psalmist praises God because He brings forth the winds out of His treasury (Psalm 134 [135]:7), but how much more should God be praised for depositing such great supplies of water in the earth.

A story is told about an uneducated African who was crossing a river in Spain between Córdoba and Castro del Río. After gazing at the rushing water, he turned to his master and said: "Flowing, flowing, and never filled up; flowing, flowing, and never ending; a great thing is God." This African with no education puts us to shame and reminds us to praise God for this blessing. Even more pointedly did the angel of the Apocalypse invite men to praise God when he flew down from heaven, crying out to the people of the earth: "Fear the Lord, and give Him honor, because the hour of His judgment is come, and adore ye Him, that made heaven and earth, the sea, and the fountains of waters" (Apocalypse 14:7).

The heavens, the stars, and the other elements that we have previously discussed do not have life. Now, seeing that things that possess life are more perfect than those which do not, they are a greater manifestation of the wisdom and providence of the Creator, and the more perfect the life, the more clearly do they reflect their Maker. God, as they say, is not penny-wise and pound-foolish. The more perfect a thing is, the greater is His care and providence over it and the more clearly does He manifest His wisdom through it.

To God alone we owe the great blessings of the fruits of the earth. By His word alone He created the plants and trees of the earth, as we read: "Let the earth bring forth the green herb, and such as may seed, and the fruit tree yielding fruit after its kind, which may have seed in itself upon the earth" (Genesis 1:11). Once spoken, the command was carried out and the earth was clothed in green and adorned with many flowers and plants and trees.

Who can describe the beauty of the fields? What can we say of such splendor? But we have the testimony of Scripture, where the holy patriarch compares the blessing and grace of the saints with the sweet aroma of a fertile field: "Behold the smell of my son is as the smell of a plentiful field, which the Lord hath blessed" (Genesis 27:27).

Who can portray the beauty of the purple violets, the white lilies, the blood-red rose? What artist could reproduce on his canvas a summer's meadow with its flowers of various hues, some yellow, some red, and others a mixture of many colors? Indeed, one cannot say what pleases him most, the color of the flower, the delicacy of its shape, or the sweet odor that comes from it. The eyes feast on the beautiful spectacle while the perfume of the flowers delights the sense of smell. Such is the grace and beauty which the Creator applies to Himself when He says: "The beauty of the fields is in Me."

Gaze upon the lily and see its dazzling whiteness. See how the slender stem rises gracefully and terminates in a chalice of lovely petals that protect and enclose grains of gold so that no harm may come to them. What human artist could ever make anything like it? The Savior Himself praised the lilies of the field when He said that not even

Solomon in all his glory was dressed as richly as one of these flowers (Matthew 6:29).

Even more amazing is the fact that the seeds scattered on the earth do not bring forth fruit unless they first die. St. Ambrose waxed eloquent on this point when he described the way in which a grain of wheat grows, using this as an example of how one can seek and find God in all things. He describes how the earth receives the grain of wheat and, like a mother, gathers the seed to her womb. Gradually the seed is changed into a sprout and ultimately becomes full-grown. When it reaches maturity, it produces a sheath or head that contains little pods wherein new seeds are formed. Thus, the cold cannot damage the seeds nor can the sun burn them with its intense heat; the wind will not blow them away nor will water damage them. The sheath also protects the grains of wheat from the birds, not only by reason of the pods that contain the seeds, but also by means of little pointed whiskers or strands that protrude from the sheath. And because the slender stem could not of itself bear the weight of the sheath of wheat, it is strengthened by a covering of leaves with which it is adorned and by the knots or knuckles that are distributed at intervals along the stem. This is not true of oats, however, for this grain does not need such protection. We see from this that the divine Creator does not fail us in those things that are necessary but neither does He make things that are useless.

The earth also produces many kinds of vegetables for our sustenance. Some are kept dry and can be used at any time during the entire year; others we eat as soon as they are ripe. Some grow under the ground and others above it, and of those that grow above the ground, some reproduce seeds within themselves, to be used for future planting. We read that the children of Israel yearned for such vegetables while crossing the desert. Here again we see divine providence, which not only provides fresh fruit in the summertime for the refreshment of the body, but also made vegetables that are to be eaten in due season. Not content with providing us with the flesh of so many animals, fish, and birds, and with a variety of fruits and abundant grains, He also gave us many kinds of vegetables so that no type of nourishment would be lacking to us. But how badly man uses these gifts! Even while he enjoys them, he does not think to raise his eyes to see the hand from which these gifts and benefits flow, not only to the good, but even to sinners.

Even though there are scantily clothed natives in desolate places that men call barbarians, there are also many civilized barbarians dressed in the costliest garments. Let us think of a traveler that stops at the home of a wealthy citizen. Suppose the rich man, without any obligation, were not only to receive the stranger as a guest and treat him with every possible kindness, but also that he seated his guest at a table laden with the choicest foods that he had in the house. Now, if after eating, the traveler should depart without bidding his host farewell or thanking him for his hospitality and generosity, what would we think of such a person? We would say that he was more of a barbarian than the most inhuman savage.

What, then, is the status of so many wealthy and powerful men who sit every day at a table laden with the countless gifts that God has provided, not for Himself nor for the angels, but for man, and yet they neither thank Him who, without any obligation on His part, has so generously provided for man, nor do they even notice it? Every day they see the proof of God's blessings but they never give a thought to His generous and magnificent providence. Who will deny that men such as these, who live in complete forgetfulness of God, are worse than barbarians? They are like the rich man in the Gospel who dined every day in great splendor, but gave not a thought to God or to the poor beggar who sat at his gate (Luke 16:21).

What shall we say of the variety of beautiful flowers, which do not serve for man's sustenance but for his delight? What other reason is there for the carnations, marigolds, lilies, irises, violets, and numerous other flowers that fill the gardens and cover the hills and fields and meadows? Consider their various colors, the beauty and artistry with which they are fashioned, the order and harmony of the leaves with which they are embellished, and the delightful scents which many of them emit. Of what service are all these things, except to give man something on which he can feast his eyes? Even more, they give joy to the soul when, in contemplating the flowers, a man can recognize the beauty of God and the great care that He has shown for us in showering us with gifts.

God is not content merely with providing us with the

necessities of life, but also for our recreation and delight. Not only did He desire that we should gaze upon the splendor of the stars on a serene night, but also that we should enjoy the sight of the multicolored flowers against the fertile valleys and green plains, like another heaven splashed with flowery stars. Such beauty serves a double purpose: on the one hand, it delights us with its loveliness and splendor; on the other hand, it arouses us to the praise of the Creator who made all these things, not for Himself or for the angels or for brute animals, but for the honest pleasure of men.

Take any one flower from among the great variety and ask: Since God does nothing without a purpose, why did He create this most beautiful and sweet-smelling flower? It is not for the sustenance of man nor for medicinal use or any other utility. Then, what other purpose can this flower have but to delight our vision with its beauty and our sense of smell with its sweet aroma? Consider also how many different kinds of flowers God created for the same purpose and how many other things He has made for the delight of the other senses. Then, the brilliance of jewels and precious stones which dazzle the eye, the music of the birds which pleases the ear, the various perfumes and herbs which captivate our sense of smell, and the infinity of savors which satisfy our sense of taste.

All of them declare to us the sweetness and benignity of the sovereign Lord who had such a regard for men that He not only created a variety of foods and other things necessary for man's sustenance, but He took special care to create many different things for man's genuine recreation. God provided for man so generously that none of the bodily senses lacks its proper object in which it can find delight. What greater proof of our Father's love for us than the gratuitous blessings He has bestowed on us?

Not content with this, God also created a variety of trees, such as the laurel, the myrtle, the cypress, the cedars, the poplar, and the ivy which adorns the walls of gardens and serves them as cover of protection. Some trees bear fruit and others are sterile, while some give nourishment to men, others to beasts. Some never lose their leaves; others change each year. Some serve only for shade and decoration, while others serve various purposes. Among the fruit-bearing trees, some give fruit for consumption in the summer, while others give fruit that can be kept for the wintertime. Here again we see a manifestation of God's generosity and providence in creating trees of various kinds so that there would be both a sufficiency and a variety of fruits.

Consider the variety of plums and apples and grapes. Not only that, but how even on the one tree, the fruit does not ripen all at once, but gradually. Thus, we see that on the fig tree some fruit ripens while the rest is yet green and, in this way, the one tree provides a supply of fruit over a longer period. But the wisdom of divine providence is still more evident in the summer fruits. In the heat and dryness of the summer, men naturally seek the refreshment of juicy fruits which the Creator has provided at that season. Nor does the fact that many men get sick on fruit

militate against God's providence, for this is not the fault of the fruit but of the intemperate man who uses God's gifts badly. In like manner, it is not the fault of the wine that many use it immoderately, but it is the fault of the one who partakes of it.

Divine wisdom manifests itself no less in the structure of the trees themselves. If a man wishes to build a house, he first prepares the foundations on which the house will be supported. Likewise, in fashioning trees, God has decreed that before the tree raises its branches into the air, it should be firmly rooted in the earth, and these roots will be in proportion to the height and breadth of the tree. The higher the tree, the deeper its roots. Once a young tree is firmly rooted, the trunk gradually thickens until it resembles a column or pillar of a building and can support the canopy of the branches with their leaves and blossoms and, later, the mature fruit. The ancients observe that in spite of the great diversity of trees and shrubs and plants, no one leaf is exactly like any other; there is always a difference in size, shape, color, or some other detail. The same is observed in regard to the diversity of human faces; there is scarcely one man who looks like another.

It is also remarkable how trees are nourished and maintained. The little hair-like strands that protrude from the roots absorb moisture from the earth and then the heat of the sun draws this moisture upward through the trunk of the tree and through all its branches. The bark of the tree serves as a protective covering over the pores of the tree through which the moisture passes. The leaves are equipped with veins similar to those in the human body. A large vein divides the leaf into two equal parts and the smaller subsidiary veins which branch off from it carry nourishment to all parts of the leaf.

Not only is the tree sustained and nourished, but it also grows to a great size because of its vegetative soul. Animals possess the powers of the vegetative soul as well as those of a sensitive soul; consequently, they are not only occupied with the sustenance and growth of the body, but even more so with functions of the external senses. Plants, however, lack a sensitive soul and therefore, their powers are concentrated on nourishment and growth. We see that men who are more given to study or contemplation have flabbier bodies because they exercise their intellectual faculties rather than their bodily members.

What of the beauty of the trees when they are laden with ripe fruit? What, for example, is more pleasing to the sight than an apple tree when its branches are weighed down with apples of different shades of color that give off such a delightful smell? Again, how beautiful is the grapevine with its copious green leaves, among which are half-concealed large clusters of grapes of various shapes and colors, like so many jewels suspended from the branches of the vine?

Nor did providence fail to take precautions to safeguard the ripe fruits. The trees have leaves not only for beauty and shade but also to protect the fruit from the heat of the sun, which would otherwise wither the fruit.

And if the fruit is especially tender, as are figs or grapes, the leaves are larger, in order to afford greater protection. However, the leaves do not cover the trees and vines like a solid blanket. Little openings are provided here and there so that the warm winds and snatches of sunlight can touch the ripening fruits.

God's providence is even more evident in the manner that the fruits of the tree are protected from greater dangers. The fruit of the tall pines, which grow in windy places or on mountain sides, would never ripen had God not fashioned the pine comb wherein each seed is placed in its own compartment and so well protected that all the fury of the winds cannot dislodge it. We see this also with chestnut trees. Their fruit becomes the food of the poor when they have no bread and they are found in mountainous places and subject to the violence and coldness of the winds. So, the chestnut is covered with a prickly husk and with two inner tunics, one very hard and the other soft. In this way the chestnuts are protected against damage from the heat of the sun and the force of the winds. Moreover, since some trees bear a fruit that is large and heavy, such as the citrus fruits, the Creator provided that the branches of such trees should be strong and thick so that they could more easily support the weight of the fruit. We see from all this that divine providence has not been wanting or wasteful in any created thing.

Finally, look at the beauty of the pomegranate. How well it manifests the artistry of the Creator! First, the Creator has covered this fruit on the outside with clothing that is made to its measure and completely encircles it to protect it from the violence of the sun and wind. The outside of this tunic or skin is hard and durable, but its inside is soft and downy so that it will not injure the tender fruit contained within. The seeds of the fruit are distributed into sections and each section is divided by a membrane more delicate than silk. Now, if any one of these quarters or sections should become spoiled, the membrane preserves the neighboring sections so that they are not contaminated. In much the same way, God divided the lobes of our brain and surrounded each with a membrane so that harm done to one section would not affect the others. Each seed of the pomegranate contains within itself a white bony substance so that its soft exterior will be better preserved and at its base it has a little stem, as thin as a thread, through which the seed receives its nourishment, in much the same way as the embryo in the womb of its mother is nourished through the umbilical cord. The seeds rest upon a white, soft substance similar to that of the inside of the skin that covers the entire fruit. Lastly, a royal crown adorns the top of the pomegranate, as if the Creator wished to designate it as the queen of all fruits. From the color of its seeds, which are as beautiful as coral, to its delicious taste and health-giving qualities, there is no fruit to compare with the pomegranate.

But why is it that men, who are so astute at analyzing human affairs, do not see the wise and loving providence that has created so beneficial and beautiful a fruit? The bride in the Song of Songs understands this much better,

for she invites the bridegroom to go forth to the vineyards to see if the flowers be ready to bring forth fruits and if the pomegranates flourish (Cant. 7:12). Speaking of the vineyard, although the vine is a small tree, its fruit is not at all insignificant. It supplies grapes for the whole year and the wine that strengthens and gladdens the heart of man. It also provides vinegar, must, and raisins. Therefore, it is fitting that the Savior should compare Himself to the vine when He says: "I am the vine; you, the branches.... As the branch cannot bear fruit of itself, unless it abides in the vine, so neither can you, unless you abide in Me" (John 15:4–5).

Since the vine is small and cannot grow to great heights, it has been provided with tendrils that attach themselves to the branches of trees and climb to the height of the tree itself. Here we have a symbol of our redemption! Imitating the vine, we creatures, who are base and

lowly in comparison with the angels, ascend on high by clinging to that cedar of Lebanon which is Christ, our Redeemer. By uniting ourselves to Him with the bonds of love we shall rise with Him and ascend to heaven with Him. St. Gregory says that since we were unable to grasp the divine greatness, God abased Himself in coming down to earth in order to lift us up and carry us on His shoulders. For by the mystery of the Incarnation human nature was ennobled and exalted above the angels.

Some trees are sterile and purely forest trees, and yet God has created them out of regard for our needs. For men need not only sustenance by way of food, but they also need houses and dwellings as a protection against the inclemency of the weather, and God has created trees suitable for this purpose. He ordained that fruit trees should usually be low and that their branches should extend outward like long arms so that the fruit could be more easily gathered. But the pine, the oak, the poplar, and other trees that were made to supply wood for building are tall and straight. Lastly, many different kinds of trees provide food for the animals that eat of their leaves and bark, supply fuel for the fire that is so necessary to men, and serve as a source of medicinal elements that are beneficial to human health.

Divine providence has shown great care for the conservation of the various species of plants. First, He provided that an abundance of seeds should be produced by each plant so that seeds would never be lacking from which a plant could be reproduced. Secondly, He endowed each seed with such power that from the smallest seed a shrub or tree is reproduced. We see proof of both of these things in the mustard seed to which the Savior referred in the Gospel parable. Each tree produces millions of seeds and each seed is capable of producing another tree that will again produce millions of seeds. A melon seed produces a vine of melons and each new melon contains numerous seeds that can again produce new melons. Or think of the seeds of an orange and how many other oranges and seeds they can produce.

How, then, can there ever be lacking a sufficiency of fruits and plants, when there is so much material from which they can be reproduced? How well God has provided for us! And when you have considered God's generosity in these things, consider also how copious was the redemption that He sent to us through the incarnation of His Son. If He was generous in providing for the preservation of plants, how much more generous and merciful has He been in restoring and sanctifying the human race? The Apostle realized this when he said that the riches of grace which the Son of God brought down to earth are incomprehensible. And Christ Himself said: "I am come that they may have life, and may have it more abundantly" (John 10:4).

6

VARIETY AND PERFECTIONS OF ANIMALS

The animals possess another and more perfect grade of life than that of the plants since they are capable of sensation and movement. And since the animals are more perfect than the plants, they give greater evidence of the divine providence of the Creator who exerts greater care over things that are more perfect.

There are books written by famous authors who so marveled at the structure of the bodies of animals and their powers of self-preservation, that they were prompted to make detailed studies of the nature and characteristics of animals. Alexander the Great, for example, even in the midst of great military enterprises which were sufficient to occupy his full time, was so anxious to know about the nature and properties of animals that he commanded hunters, fishermen, mountaineers, and shepherds of Greece and Asia to give Aristotle a complete account of all that they knew so that he could write his famous books on the animal world.

But how much more does the religious man gain from the consideration of these matters, since they raise him above all creation? This is why Jeremiah says: "Let not the wise man glory in his wisdom, and let not the strong man glory in his strength, and let not the rich man glory in his riches; but let he that boasts boast in this, that he understands and knows Me, for I am the Lord that exercise mercy, and judgment, and justice in the earth" (Jeremiah 9:23).

God supplies for the lack of reasoning power in animals by implanting in them certain natural inclinations and instincts, so that in many things animals act as if they possessed perfect reasoning power. If one remembers this fact, these things will not seem incredible to him. In creating the animals God gave them whatever was necessary for their conservation. So, St. Thomas Aquinas states that animals are like instruments in the hands of God who, as their first and principal cause, moves them in accordance with their natures through the natural inclinations and instincts which He implanted in them when He created them (I IIæ q. 1, a2). Moreover, God did not merely provide for the needs of the animals themselves; He also manifests His glory through them, and this is more evident as the marvels He performs are greater and more numerous.

So really, no one should think any of these matters are incredible, for God is the efficient cause who makes all these things possible and they are all the more credible as they give greater testimony of His glory, which is the final cause of all creation, both visible and invisible.

What men do for their preservation; the animals likewise do for theirs. To select one example from many others, consider the skill with which the swallow builds her nest. Just as the mason, when he wishes to cover a wall with adobe, mixes straw with the clay to give the adobe the necessary consistency, so the swallow does the same thing in the building of her nest. And in all those things required for the care of her young ones, the swallow acts the same as any being that possesses an intellect.

The Creator gave man an intellect so that out of the infinite number of things required for his conservation, he could discover or devise whatever is necessary for his well-being. But God does not need to preserve the life of animals in the same way, for although they lack the power of reasoning, He has implanted in them those natural inclinations and instincts whereby they can do all that they would do if they had an intellect, and sometimes they do things much more perfectly than man. Working through instinct, they have greater certitude, more infallibility, more regularity than men do in in their own preservation. Moreover, animals are so adept at recognizing those things that are beneficial or medicinal and in sensing the changes in the temperature and weather that men frequently have to learn these things from them. God has here manifested the greatness of His power and wisdom and providence, for although the species of animals are innumerable, in none of them, however small, did he omit or overlook a single detail.

God in His infinite goodness has created animals for the service of man and has provided the animals themselves with all that is necessary for their own conservation and well-being. Thus, animals have the power to nourish themselves, defend themselves, cure themselves of sickness, and procreate their offspring.

God has created a variety of foods proportionate to the different kinds of animals for their preservation and nourishment. Some live on meat, others on blood, some on herbs, others on grain, and still others on insects of the earth or air. And since there is an endless variety of animals, both great and small, God has provided such a variety of nourishment that there is no animal, however small, that lacks food for its sustenance. Thus, the Psalmist says that God has provided food for all flesh (Psalm 135 [136]:25), and gives beasts their food (Psalm 146:9).

This is especially evident in the case of those birds that do not feed on plants. During the month of May, when there is as yet no wheat, no barley, no flax, and no other grain in the fields, we see so many swallows in Spain that every church and house and farm is swarming with them. What serves as food for the mouths of so many parents and young ones at a time when there is no grain on which they can feed? Only the Lord who provides for them knows what they eat. Christ Himself uses this

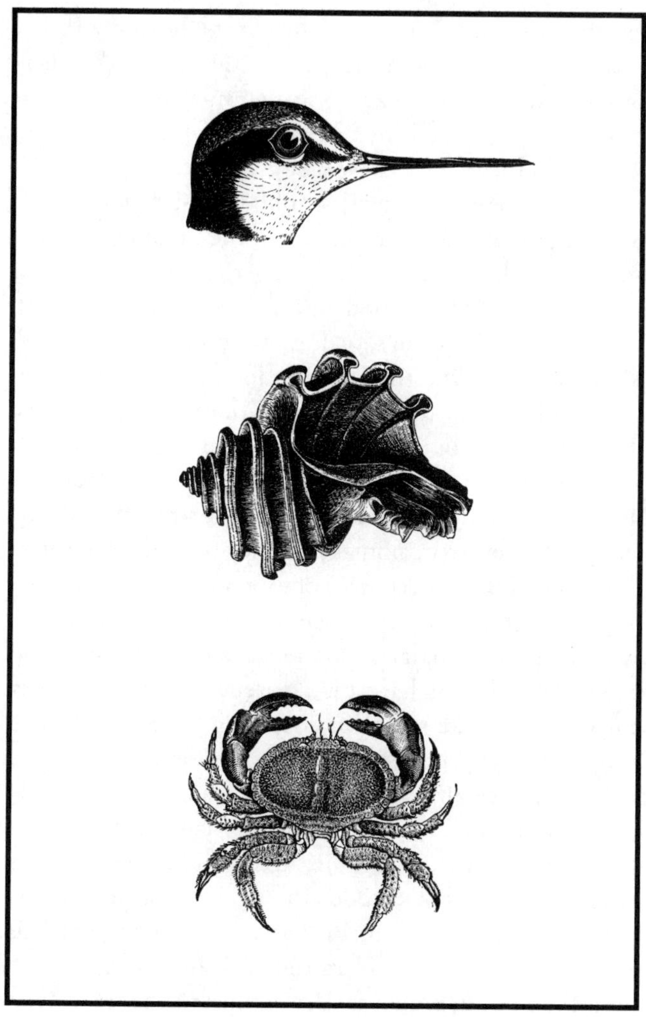

example to arouse our confidence in the heavenly Father when He says: "Behold the birds of the air, for they neither sow, nor do they reap, nor gather into barns; and your heavenly Father feeds them. Are not you of much more value than they?" (Matthew 6:26)

To ensure that animals would have sufficient nourishment, the Creator gave them all the faculties, powers, and senses they need to find their food. He gave them eyes to seek out their food and the power of movement, by means of feet, wings, or fins, to approach their food. Many animals have their bodies inclined earthward, in order to be closer to the source of their food. And since there are many animals that feed upon the weaker species, the Creator fashioned their bodies in such a way that they could defend themselves against the strength and violence of those fiercer animals, lest they be killed and eaten. Consequently, some are swift of foot, some have the speed of wings, some have a hard defensive shell, such as oysters and clams, or strong arms for attack, such as lobsters and crabs, while others have the astuteness to hide in their burrows or to take refuge in flocks and herds and thus be assisted by many against the attacks of a few.

Now, since animals, like men, are subject to sickness, God gave them a natural instinct for curing themselves and seeking remedies against disease. They also possess instinctive knowledge about the danger that may come to them from other animals that are their enemies. This is why the sheep flees from the wolf but does not flee from the mastiff, which is very similar to the wolf. God also gave the animals the faculty of anticipating changes in the weather that would prove harmful to them, so that they can prepare themselves against the changes of seasons. Thus, the birds move from place to place, spending the winters in the south where it is warm and then returning to the north in the summer. We also see that animals have a sense of providing for the future by storing up food in the summer for nourishment during the winter.

God has also taken care of the conservation of the species of animals. At certain times of the year animals are vehemently inclined to satisfy their instinct for the preservation of the species. And although the inclination for the procreation of young ones is extremely vehement in animals at certain times in the year, when this period is passed, the animals return to their former tranquility and repose. Then the male and female animals can again associate and live together in all honesty and temperance. The temperance of animals outside the season of procreation is a proof of the effects of original sin in man, because many men are extremely lax in observing the law of temperance.

How solicitous are the animals in the nourishment and defense of their offspring! Consider the care which birds have for their young. God seems to have given birds the greatest love for their young ones because they have the greatest difficulty in caring for them. Birds must remain light in weight if they are to fly, and therefore the Creator did not equip them with organs for producing milk nor weigh them down with the milk like other animals. So, it is necessary for birds to share the food that they have gathered with their young at the cost of much effort. And since birds have greater difficulty in finding food and feeding their young, the Creator gave them a stronger parental love, for love can do all things and conquer all things, and to the one who loves it is considered no hardship at all but rather a delight. Sacrifice is easy for one who loves. So, St. Bernard tells us: "Let us love Christ, my brothers, and then everything difficult will become easy."

It is also remarkable to observe the facility which birds have for building their nests. As a rule, they are made just like little baskets which easily accommodate the number of their young. Inside the nest they place soft grass or downy feathers so that the tender little fledglings will not be wounded by the roughness of the nest. What more could the parent birds do even if they had the use of reason? And in order that the little ones will not dirty the nest with their excrement, they are placed at the edge of the nest to purge themselves and later the parent bird cleans the nest with its beak, a masterly organ which serves not only to build the nest but also to keep it clean.

Some birds and other animals are much hunted but are too weak to defend themselves well. Divine providence has given them a remarkable fertility so that the species would be preserved, as we see in the case of doves and rabbits, which bring forth their young almost every month, and the partridges, which sometimes lay as many as twenty eggs. Moreover, all animals have either defensive or offensive weapons. Some have horns, some have claws, and others have teeth. The animals that are not strongly armed have the astuteness and speed to protect themselves from the violence of the strong. For example, the hare and the deer which, for their size, are the fastest and lightest of animals. The animals instinctively know how to make the best use of their various weapons, as we see in the case of the calf, which tries to attack or wound with that part of the body where its horns will later be developed.

Animals know by instinct the force of the more powerful and harmful animals. Thus, the little birds tremble at the sight of a hawk. Animals also know which food is healthy for them and which will do them harm and they will eat from the one but never touch the other, however hungry they may be. The Creator has taught them those things which men could never know except by study or experiment. He also knew that since the animals lack the power of reasoning, they would be unable to seek and find clothing for the body and covering for the feet. Consequently, He provided all animals with these things as soon as they were born and sometimes even before birth. Some he provided with feathers, some with hides and skin, others with wool, some with scales, others with shells. Some animals change their clothes every year but others keep the same covering all their lives, and it never gets old or torn. Lastly, although the animals do not have the power of speech, they are able to manifest their anger, courage, meekness, hunger, and pain by various sounds. So, the fledgling birds make known their hunger by peeping and in this way, they beg their parents for food.

Not content with having given the animals the means

whereby to preserve themselves and procreate their species, He also gave them every kind of happiness and delight which they are capable of enjoying. The Psalmist speaks of this when he says: "The eyes of all hope in You, O Lord, and You give them meat in due season. You open Your hand, and fill with blessing every living creature" (Psalm 144:15-16). These words signify that every animal enjoys happiness proportionate to its nature.

When we hear the singing of the swallow, the nightingale, or the canary, we should realize that if such music is delightful to our ears, it is no less pleasing to the bird that is singing. We also notice that the bird does not sing when it is sad or when the weather is dismal and dreary. When we see young calves briskly scamper from one place to another, or young sheep withdraw some distance from the flock in order to romp with one another, we know that this is a sign of their happiness and contentment. And when we see kittens or puppies playfully fight one another, rolling over and over and biting each other without doing any injury, is this not a sign of their happiness and joy? The same thing is true of the schools of fish as they swim to and fro or the flocks of birds as they fly after each other in circles, singing with delight.

From all this we can see what the great Dionysius meant when he said that God made all things like unto Himself, so far as their natures and capacities would permit. Just as God is happiness and joy, so also, He desired that all creatures should enjoy happiness in due measure. So, He did not rest content with giving animals the means for self-preservation, but He also wanted them to imitate Himself in happiness and contentment.

What a great testimony this is to the goodness and generosity of God. O immense goodness of God! O ineffable tenderness! That You, Lord, should have acted in this way toward rational creatures, who are able to recognize Your blessings and give thanks to You, would not be unduly strange. But to do so for creatures that can neither know You nor praise You nor thank You for Your gifts and blessings, this declares to us the greatness of Your nobility, as well as Your goodness and liberality toward Your creatures. Out of Your gratuitous love You have given them every blessing, without expecting any return or thanks. Here we are given to understand what You must have reserved both in this life and in the life to come for those who serve and love You, since You have been so generous to insensible creatures that know You not.

The earth, air, and sea are filled with all Your marvels, Lord, so that the Psalmist exclaims: "O Lord our Lord, how admirable is Your name in the whole earth! For Your magnificence is elevated above the heavens.... I will behold Your heavens, the works of Your fingers; the moon and the stars which You has founded. What is man that You are mindful of him, or the son of man that You visit him? You have made him a little less than the angels; You have crowned him with glory and honor and have set him over the works of Your hands. You have subjected all things under his feet, all sheep and oxen, moreover the beasts also of the fields, the birds of the air and the fishes of the sea.... O Lord our Lord, how admirable is Your name in the whole earth!" (Psalm 8).

7

GOD'S CARE OF THE ANIMAL KINGDOM

How numerous are the creatures through which the divine Majesty manifests Himself to man! How different are the ways in which His wisdom and providence shine forth! Truly, not only the larger animals but even the small and lowly reflect the divine attributes. St. Jerome, observing this same wonder, says that we marvel at the Creator not only in the making of the heavens and the earth, of the sun and the oceans, and of great animals like elephants and lions, but also in the creation of such tiny insects as ants, mosquitoes, flies, and many others whose bodies we know better than their names. No less in these little insects than in the large animals do we venerate the wisdom and power of Him who made them.

God's artistry in making these little things seemed more admirable to St. Augustine than the creation of greater things. "I am more amazed," he says, "at the lightness of the insects that fly than the greatness of the beasts that walk and I marvel more at the work of the ants than at that of the camels." Aristotle also states in his treatise on the animals that there is no animal so lowly and insignificant that we cannot find in it some cause for admiration.

Ancient authors give an example of this when they speak of the mosquito, which was more a cause of wonder to them than the elephant. In large animals there is an abundance of material for various parts and organs, but in these little insects, which are almost nothing, what harmony of parts, what great concentration of power, and what perfection is to be found. Consider the various senses of the mosquito: the eyes, the taste, the sense of smell, and that fearful stinger which is so large in proportion to the rest of the body. Then there is the delicacy of the wings and the length of the legs. Men marvel at the bodies of elephants, which are strong enough to pull down towers and castles, but the truth of the matter is that in no creature is nature more perfect and compact than in these little insects.

Hugh of St. Victor observes that there are many admirable things, and for different reasons—some, are great, and others are small. This is why we are astonished at giants among men, at whales among fish, at the ostrich among birds, and at the elephant among animals. Of the smaller creatures, we marvel at those that have the smallest bodies; the tiny moth, the mosquito, the ant, and other creatures of this kind. Should you marvel more at the teeth of the wild boar or those of the moth, the wings of an eagle or those of the mosquito, the head of a horse or that of a grasshopper, the legs of an elephant or those of a tortoise? In the former animals you are amazed at their size, while in the latter, at their smallness. Yet we find nothing in the larger animals that is not duplicated in the smaller ones.

Let us now consider one of the smallest of all animals: the ant. After the wounds and loss that came to man because of original sin, the principal remedy that remained to him was a hope in divine mercy, as David signifies when he says: "In peace in the selfsame will I sleep, and I will rest, for You, O Lord, have singularly settled me in hope" (Psalm 4:9-10). We have many motives for strengthening this virtue, yet I do not think I am wrong in saying that this virtue is greatly animated by a consideration of the remarkable faculties and powers that the Creator has given to a creature as insignificant and lowly as the ant.

Now, the majority of animals are concerned only with the present and pay little heed to the past or the future. On the other hand, this little creature is very concerned with what is to come, for it provides in the summer for the coming of winter. It would please God if men would imitate the ants in this regard by storing up a provision of good works in this life in order to have happiness in the next. Thus, Solomon warns us to perform good works

in earnest, for in the next life there will be no opportunity for work and merit (Ecclesiastes 9:10). But if men do not imitate the foresight of the ants, they will fulfill the prophecy uttered by the same Solomon: "He that gathers in the harvest, is a wise son; but he that snorts in the summer, is the son of confusion" (Proverbs 10:5). So also, the five foolish virgins were baffled because they did not trim their lamps and fill them with oil, as we read in the Gospel (Matthew 25:1-13).

Without any tools or materials, the ants build a storehouse or granary beneath the earth where they can preserve their food supply. The passages leading to the storeroom are not made in a straight line, but with many twists and curves, so that if an enemy insect enters the portals, it cannot easily find the ants or rob the storehouse. And with the same mouth with which they make their homes, they carry out the sand and dirt to place it in a heap outside the entrance.

When they go to the fields to gather wheat or grain, the larger ants climb up the stalk, break off the seeds, and throw them down to the smaller ants who, without any instrument except their mouths, strip off the husks or shell. When the grain is cleaned and stripped, they carry it to the storehouse, walking backwards and dragging the grain with their mouths. Then, in comparison with the size of their bodies, ants have more strength than any other creature. It would be almost impossible to find a man who could walk around for a whole day, carrying another man on his shoulders, but an ant can carry a grain of wheat that weighs more than four ants and he can stay at this task not only for a whole day, but all night, too.

And what prevents the grains of wheat from sprouting when they are placed under the ground, especially when it rains? What measures would man take to prevent this, granted that the grain must be kept in the same place for some time? For my part, I admit that I would not know what to do; the ant knows, seeing that he was taught by another Master. It sterilizes the grain of wheat by eating away that part where the sprout would normally appear. But what protects the grain from humidity, which is the mother of plant corruption? How is it that the grains do not putrefy when kept in the damp earth? The ants have a remedy for this also, for on sunny days they carry their deposit into the sunshine and when it is dried out, they put it back in storage. In this way food can be preserved for the whole year.

Not only do the ants store small items of food, but

if the things are large, they break them into little pieces so that they can drag or carry them. Another remarkable thing is that when they are scurrying from place to place in search of food and carrying their burdens to and fro, they pay no attention to each other. But on certain days, known only to themselves, they gather together into family reunions and will not admit other ants to the gathering. They are very partial to sweet things and have such an acute sense of smell that even if the sweets are well hidden or placed at a great height, they will search for it and find it.

Here again we see with what great confidence man should seek from God the remedy for all his needs. Let him place his trust in God and say to Him: "You, O Lord, who have given so many remarkable powers to the insignificant ant for the conservation of its life, how could You ever be unmindful of man whom You created in Your image and likeness, destined for a share in Your glory, and redeemed with the precious blood of Your Son? If You have such great care of little things, how much greater must be Your care of man? What does it matter whether an ant lives or dies? How much more important it is that man should live, to whom You gave life through Your blood?"

Let man rid himself completely of his sins, seeing that they are, as Isaiah says, a wall that divides man from God (Isaiah 59:2). Let him be assured that God will have a greater care for him than He does for the ant, because man is a far nobler creature than the ant. God is not, as the saying goes, one who gathers ashes and scatters wheat. Whatever He does for the ant is not for the ant itself, but to make known to man His wisdom and providence and by this example to arouse man's confidence in Him. Likewise, the Gospel reminds us of His care of the birds, which neither sow nor reap, in order to arouse our confidence in God.

The spider is of no use to human life but nevertheless has received no few powers from the Creator for the preservation of its own life. Spiders are nourished on the blood of flies and other insects. In order to catch their prey, they weave webs that have threads more delicate than those of the finest fabrics. For this purpose, they need no foreign substance, but draw the threads from their own stomachs. The web serves to conceal the small holes or chinks where the spider lies in wait like a highwayman to leap out and attack its victim. When a fly innocently lands on the web and gets entangled in it, the spider approaches quickly and binds the fly on all sides. When this has been done, it leaps upon the fly and kills it.

Other spiders make their webs in the air, attaching the threads to the branches of trees or bushes. Then they proceed to weave a perfectly meshed net, similar to that of a fisherman to await the arrival of their game, poised at the center of the web where all the threads meet and where they can feel the movement of any thread on which the fly lands. If the spider were to stand on a single strand at some distance from the center, it would not feel the movement of the web.

Other spiders make their nests just beneath the surface of the earth and line it with a texture of interwoven threads, so that if the earth should crumble, it will not fill up their house. They then make a large stopper or cover to fill the entrance to their nest. Taking a piece of dirt, they cover it with many threads, so that it fits perfectly into the mouth of the nest and can scarcely be distinguished from the surrounding earth. What is still more admirable is that the threads that are woven around the pellet of earth are then connected with the other threads and webs that adorn the whole nest, thus making a hinge for the cover of the nest. Who could have taught this insect how to seal its house and even attach a door to it, except He who created the spider?

Aristotle states in his treatise on animals that the smallest creatures manifest more of a similarity to intelligent activity than do other animals. The lowlier and more insignificant the animals, the better they manifest to us the omnipotence and wisdom of the Creator who has placed such extraordinary powers in such tiny bodies. Likewise, they better manifest the aid of divine providence that does not fail even the little and insignificant creatures in those things necessary for their preservation. How much greater will be His care and provision for larger creatures if He is so solicitous about things that are small?

God is so admirable in His creatures that if we could contemplate the structure of the body of each one of them and the faculties that they have for their preservation and provision, we would never cease to marvel at the immense majesty and wisdom that formed them. The truth of this statement is readily seen in the animals which we have already considered, but there are two other small creatures that to my mind are more remarkable than any of the rest: the silkworm and the bee.

Is it not a thing of great wonder that a creature as small as a silkworm can spin threads so delicate and beautiful that all the art and ingenuity of the human mind have never been able to duplicate them? Is it not a marvel that the Creator has given this little worm the power to manufacture the material for the elegant robes with which nobles, grand ladies, kings, and emperors are clothed? There is no land so uncivilized or so far distant that its kings and rulers do not strive to obtain the material that is made by these little worms.

Silkworms come from tiny eggs that are hatched in the sun or by the body heat of the parent. Within the short space of three days the eggs are hatched. From the beginning the little worms have all the faculties required for their existence. St. Basil made use of this fact to teach us about the general resurrection, for He who can give life to such a small egg in so short a time, can also give life to the dust and bones of our bodies, wherever they may be.

The new-born worms have voracious appetites and the noise they make while their little teeth bite and chew their food is like the patter of raindrops on the roof. After eating for several days, they go to sleep, while the food is gradually changed into their bodies, which rapidly increase in size. This procedure takes place three times, after which the worms are grown to full size and they stop eating. Then, they find a suitable branch and begin to spin their threads. When they have made a network of threads on a branch, they proceed to build their cocoon in the center of it. Weaving threads very closely and tightly, they construct a wall as strong and firm as if it were made of parchment. And as men whitewash the walls of a building so that they will be smooth and beautiful, so the silkworm paints the inside of the cocoon with its snout and makes it watertight.

This is a particular manifestation of God's providence, for if it were otherwise, the work of the silkworm would be of no use to man. When the cocoon is thrust into boiling water, the outer silken threads are easily disentangled and separated from one another. At the same time, however, the boiling water kills the worm inside the cocoon and this is the reward it gets for its labors. Nevertheless, those worms that are to be used for the procreation of the species do not suffer this fate. Not desiring to be imprisoned in their own house, they make a small opening in the cocoon with their mouths, and at the proper time they come forth as a kind of butterfly. The male and female remain together for four days and then the male dies. After depositing her eggs, the female also dies.

Silkworms were clearly created by divine providence only for that one function and after they have finished their task they die at the appointed time. The Creator has made these little creatures simply and solely for the benefit of mankind. Once their work is completed their life comes to an end. It is as if the little silkworm would say to man: "I was not born for myself nor do I live for myself, but for you; therefore, when I have finished my service, I leave you."

In this way, God has provided us with clothing made not only from the wool of sheep and the furs of other animals, but from fine and delicate silks. The threads of the cocoon are finer than hair but they can be woven into durable cloth. A little worm that is hatched in a few days and lives only for a few months is used by God to produce a work so delicate and precious that all the genius of man cannot duplicate it.

What shall we say now of the bees? They provide us with delicious and salutary honey which is used to sweeten foods or serves as a remedy for certain illnesses. They also give us the wax from which we make the candles to be used in churches, processions, and funerals, as well as for light and ornament on the tables of nobility. Yet all these benefits come from an insect that is little larger than a fly.

But if we are amazed at the benefits that come to us from the bees, we should be even more astonished at the order and unity they observe in their work and manner of life. Anyone who has studied or observed bees knows that they live in well-ordered colonies under the rule of a queen and with nobility and officials who perform special duties, that they have arms for attack and punishments for those who do not do what they ought, and that each one receives what is due to him by way of merit.

The life of the bees may be compared to that of a religious community of strict observance. First of all, the bees have their prelate or superior whom they obey. They live together without any private possessions, but all things are had in common. Offices and duties are assigned to each one and punishments and penances are meted out to the guilty. All of them eat together at the same time and at night there is a signal for silence which is strictly observed. Again, in the morning they have another signal for rising and those laborers are punished who do not start work promptly. They have watchmen who stand on duty to guard the hive and see that the drones do not eat the honey. Porters are assigned to the entrance of the hive so that no one can come in and steal the honey. Lastly, they have lay brothers to carry food and water and perform other menial tasks.

The sovereign Artist arranged all these things so harmoniously that they cause great admiration in all who contemplate them. It is written of the Queen of Sheba that when she saw the splendor and order of the house of Solomon, she was overwhelmed to find everything so well arranged by the talent and intelligence of so great a king. However, it is not to be wondered at that a man so far superior to others in wisdom should do things worthy of admiration. But that such little creatures as the bees should manifest so well-ordered a life and should do things so wisely, that is truly something to awaken our admiration. Sadly, the fact that we see these things around us every day lessens our admiration.

8

THE WONDERS OF BEES

We have observed the magnificence of the greater animals as well as the masterful order, care, and arrangement of the tiniest animals. Now, to see how many marvelous things witness the glory and brilliance of the creator, let us look again to the bee. The bee reflects the workings of a well-ordered society. Now, although man does many of these things through the light of reason with which he has been endowed, God's smallest creatures perform many of the same functions far better than man himself, even though they lack the use of reason. Few things better illustrate this than the workings of the humble bee. In all of this, let us remember that God did all this not merely for its own sake, but rather, to manifest His greatness and providence. If we know these things, let us be all the more ready to honor and reverence Him.

Bees have a queen whom they obey and follow wherever she goes. And as the rulers of nations have royal insignia, such as the crown and scepter by which they are distinguished from their subjects, so the Creator has distinguished the queen bee by giving it a larger and more beautiful body than the others. Whereas men mark royalty by designing insignia, nature herself has marked out the queen of the bees.

Into each swarm of bees are born three or four queens, so that if one should die or come to harm there will always be a queen. But the bees seem to know that they must not have more than one ruler and therefore they kill all but one of the queens. However much the queens may regret doing this, the love of peace overcomes sorrow, for they know that such a procedure is necessary if they are to avoid war and a divided house.

Aristotle states that since it is bad to have a multitude of leaders, the republic of this universe has but one ruler, God. The bees never learned this from Aristotle, but they realize the danger that comes from having many rulers.

Once the queen has been chosen, the bees begin to construct and furnish their home. First, they cover the walls of the beehive with a wax-like substance made from very bitter plants, for they know that the honey which they are to make is very much sought after by other animals and if they cover the hive with this offensive substance, disappointed intruders will turn away from bitter taste and will desist from further harm. For the same reason, two or three columns of wax nearest the entrance are left empty so that the thief will not find any honey to satisfy his taste.

They then proceed to make little individual houses or cells within the hive. They first construct a grand and magnificent home for the queen bee, in conformity with her royal dignity, and they encircle it with a kind of fence for greater safety and security. Then they make their own homes—the cells of the honeycomb where they lay their eggs, provide for their young, and deposit their honey. Each little cell is exactly the same, having six sides, and is perfectly proportioned, although the bees have no rule or plane or any instruments other than their mouths and legs to fashion the cells. A man would not know which one he should be more amazed at; the perfection of the work or the way in which it is carried out. The bees also make houses for their servants, the drones, but they are somewhat smaller in size.

Once the house is constructed, the bees proceed to make preparations for their labor, and the first thing they do is to assign tasks to various members of the hive. The oldest bees, who are veterans retired from labor, accompany the queen bee so that she will be more honored and have greater authority. Those next in age, who are more experienced with the work, are assigned to the making of honey. The youngest bees go forth into the fields to gather the nectar from which the honey and the wax are to be made.

These carrier bees cover the fleshy part of the thighs (which is rough so that the bees will not lose their load in flight) with the material from the flowers. Then they use their mouths to load their front legs with more nectar and return to the hive with four loads of material. When they reach the hive, other bees are assigned to unload the nectar that has been brought from the fields and meadows. A third group of bees then brings the material to those who are engaged in making wax, placing the load at the bottom of the honeycomb. Other bees are at the hand of the wax-makers to supply the material as it is needed, while another group is engaged in polishing and smoothing out the walls of the cells that have already been made. Some bees are assigned to bring food and others carry water to those who are working inside the hive. They carry the water either in their mouths or on the tiny hairs of their body so that, returning to the hive all damp with moisture, they can quench the thirst of the laborers.[1]

The queen bee presides over this. She walks through her domains to examine the works of her subjects and to encourage them by her royal presence, but she herself never applies herself to the work. She was not born to serve, but to be served, as befits a queen. In her company are the older bees that make up her cortege.

If the bees must move to another locality, they do not

[1] Editor's note: The author here, makes no distinction between different sort of bees, even though these were known in his time. He is also ambiguous about the "material" which they carry. The material which is on their bodies is pollen, while the nectar is taken into their stomach by means of the proboscis, but this detail was not known until the advent of microscopes a century later.

take a step without their queen. In the process of moving, they all surround her so that she is well concealed and all try to be as close to her as possible and to perform all manner of services for her. If the queen is old and cannot fly easily, they carry her. Wherever the queen bee rests, there all her followers rest. If she should leave them or be separated from them, they seek her out with the greatest diligence and bring her back to her subjects. Whether or not the queen bee has a stinger, she surely has no use for one, since it is beneath her royal dignity to execute or to inflict punishment personally.[2] Bees are loyal to their queen. If she dies, they all surround her to keep vigil and they will neither eat nor drink. If they are not taken from her, they will die with her.

The creator did not neglect to provide the bee with some kind of defense. Indeed, in proportion to the size of its body, there is no weapon more powerful than that of the bee: the stinger with which it can kill or wound those that try to harm it. Since the honey they provide is a treasure desired by so many other creatures, there is good reason why the bees should have the means to protect that treasure. For this reason, they keep vigil at the door of the hive so that nothing can harm the hive or the bees without being resisted as strongly as possible.

The bees do not go out to the meadows all year round, but only when the flowers are in bloom. In the time of snow and frost the bees stay in their house and

---

2 Editor's note: Today it is known that queen bees actually do have a stinger, and this is used to kill off rival queens as they hatch.

busy themselves through the winter months with tasks within the hives. Moreover, they do not go farther than sixty paces from the hive without sending their scouts ahead to look over the land and to report what type of pasture is there. Sometimes one swarm of bees will fight against another over a meadow or, if there is a lack of nourishment, they will try to rob the food from others, arranged almost like an army.

All that we have said up to this point gives evidence of the way in which the bees imitate the prudence and actions of men. And if we are amazed that such little creatures should so closely imitate men, how much more should we be amazed that they seem to know some of the things that men do not know. The bees know when there will be storms and rain even before they happen. At such times they do not go afar to gather nectar, but remain buzzing around the entrance to the hive. And when the caretaker of the bees sees this, he warns other men that there will be a change in weather.

But what causes the greatest astonishment in this matter of the bees is the production of honey, to which all their other talents are ordained. We know how many instruments and how much care are required for the making of jams and preserves. But I ask you, what instruments does this little creature have? And yet, it makes a sweet preserve from the nectar drawn from flowers.

Who taught this little creature such an alchemy whereby it can transform one substance into another? Let all the chefs, bakers and cooks join together with all

their instruments, skill, and knowledge and let them try to change flowers into honey. Not only has man been unable to effect such a transformation, but neither does he know what causes this change. Yet foolish men will spend their time in scrutinizing the mysteries of the heavens and miss the significance of those things that happen every day before their very eyes.

It is also amazing to think that from the load that the bees carry back to the hive, part is used for making honey and another part for wax. How can they, from one and the same material, make substances that are so different?

And if the flowers provide two different substances, who taught the bees how to distinguish one from the other? Who taught them to use the one part for honey and the other for wax?

Give thanks to God for the grandeur of His power and wisdom manifested in the beehive. O God, how wonderful and admirable You are in all Your works, both of nature and of grace! Yet, this should not cause us astonishment, for both the one and the other have You as their Author. They are both the children of the same Father, and for that reason do they have so many points of similarity. In the order of grace, we see that sometimes You select the weakest instruments to do wonderful things. With twelve fishermen You converted the world! With the strength of a single woman You crushed the power of the Assyrians! With the footmen of the princes of Israel You vanquished the Syrian army! With a stone and a sling, You enabled a shepherd boy to conquer a heavily-armed giant! And, with the jawbone of a donkey You gave Samson the power to kill no less than a thousand Philistines. This same disposition of things that You observe in the order of grace, You also observe in the things of nature, for You ordain that these two lowly creatures should provide kings and nobles with the costliest vestments and the sweetest of foods. Indeed, the lowlier and more insignificant the creatures and the more excellent their works, so much the more do they manifest to us the greatness of Your glory.

9

WONDERS OF THE HUMAN BODY

Man is a microcosm, or a universe in miniature, a meditation on which leads us to as profound an appreciation of God as does a meditation on the entire universe.

But first, we should recall that the beginning and basis of all our blessings is a knowledge and appreciation of God. No matter how numerous the truths we may learn about God, the one which is of utmost importance for our salvation and which gives us the greatest consolation is that of His divine providence. This attribute includes and embraces three others, namely, God's goodness, wisdom, and omnipotence.

All that we have said gives clear testimony of divine

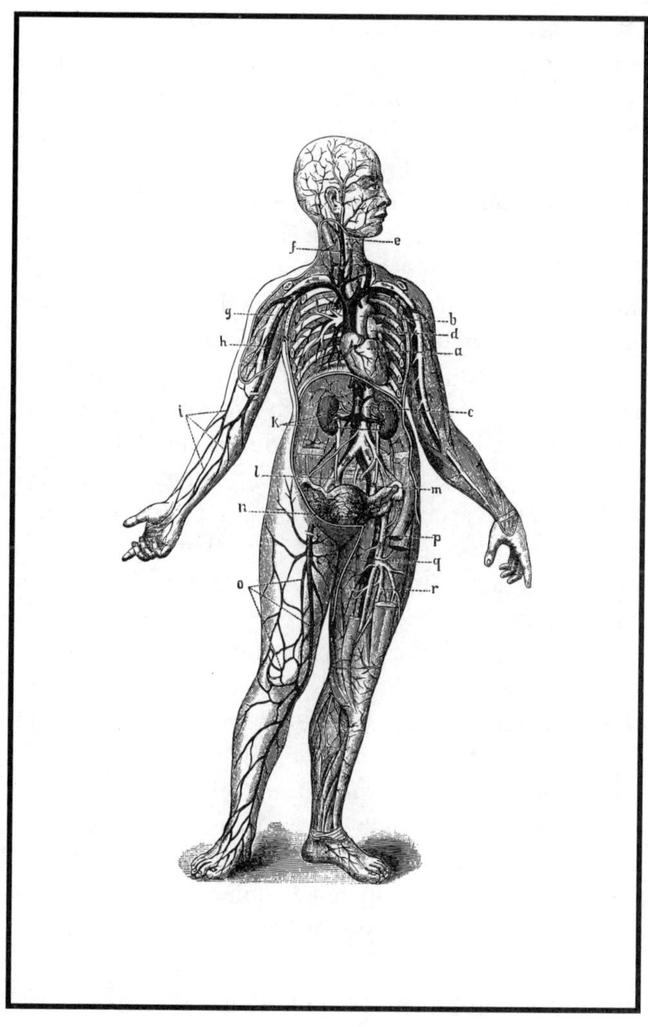
e
f
g
b
d
h
a
i
c
k
l
m
n
p
q
o
r

providence and the three divine attributes that are intimately connected with it. The same will be seen when we consider man. The reason why man is called a microcosm is because everything found in the greater universe is also found in some way in man. Man possesses being, as do all the natural elements. He possesses life, as do plants, as well as sensation, as do the animals. He has understanding and free will, as do the angels. For that reason, St. Gregory calls man "every creature" because in man the nature and properties of all created things are to be found.

God created man on the sixth day, after He had created all other things, for He wished to make man a compendium of all that He had previously made. Much the same thing is done by those who, at the end of a detailed account, place a summary or schema of that which has been treated previously in many pages. For that reason, we can more quickly and more easily see in man the traces of the divine perfections than if we were to scan the vast reaches of creation, which would take a long time. It is just as map makers are wont to do when they make charts and maps wherein, they indicate the principal parts and nations of the world so that in a brief glance one can obtain a comprehensive view of the entire earth.

In the tiny seed of an orange, for example, He placed the power to become an orange tree, and in the kernel of the acorn, the potentiality of becoming a mighty oak. But these things are very insignificant when compared with the power that He has placed in the material used for the formation of a human body. From the seed of a plant come the roots, trunk, and branches of the tree or shrub, with their leaves and fruit. Yet, from the substance used in the conception of a human being a variety of members of the human body come, such as bones, veins, arteries, nerves, and numerous organs. The various parts of the human body are so well adapted to the ends of human life that if a man observes all the particular uses and functions and providential benefits which they impart, he will be amazed at the wisdom and providence of the Creator who could produce such a variety of effects from such a simple substance.

There is nothing about the human body that does not cry out continually: "Who but God could have done this?" Who but God could have fashioned the womb of a woman as a fleshly house for the unborn child? Everything about the human body proclaims that it is a work fashioned by infinite wisdom. It is said that there are more than three hundred bones in the human body, so that on each side of the body there are approximately one hundred and fifty bones. Moreover, each bone has ten properties: a certain shape, position, connection with others, hardness, blandness, and so forth.[1]

Three marvelous characteristics are worthy of special consideration regarding the bones of the human body. The

[1] Editor's note: de Granada takes most of his information from the Roman doctor Galen, who was the standard authority for over a thousand years. Galen was not able to dissect human bodies due to Roman law, and often counted one bone as two; thus, he multiplied the count far higher than it actually is. The first major challenge to Galen came from Andreas Vesalius, with his work De Humani Corporis Fabrica. In modern anatomy we now know that there are 206 bones in a human adult.

first is the connection and interlacing of the various bones with each other, so that one fits perfectly into another. The second is the likeness between the bones on each side of the body, both as to size and the ten properties. Consequently, as the bones of the hand grow, the matching bones on the other side of the body likewise grow, so that there is no disproportion in the size of the two hands. The same thing is true of the ribs and the bones of the arms, legs, and feet.

The third marvel, which is more astonishing than the other two, is the shape and properties of each bone in the human body, and how each is fashioned to serve the office for which it was made. We can demonstrate this marvel by means of the things of art, which imitate nature. We see that the carpenter uses a saw, a hatchet, a plane, a level, and other such tools. We see also how well-proportioned and how well built these instruments are for their job. We find this same quality to an even higher degree of perfection in the bones of the human body. They are so well proportioned and suited to the functions for which they were made that all the intelligence of men and angels could not improve upon their perfection.

But the marvel does not stop here. What we have said of the proportion and likeness of the bones on each side of the body is also true of the muscles and ligaments that surround the bones, and the nerves and veins and arteries of each side of the body. All these things are instruments necessary for the preservation of our life and are very well suited to the functions for which they were made, so that

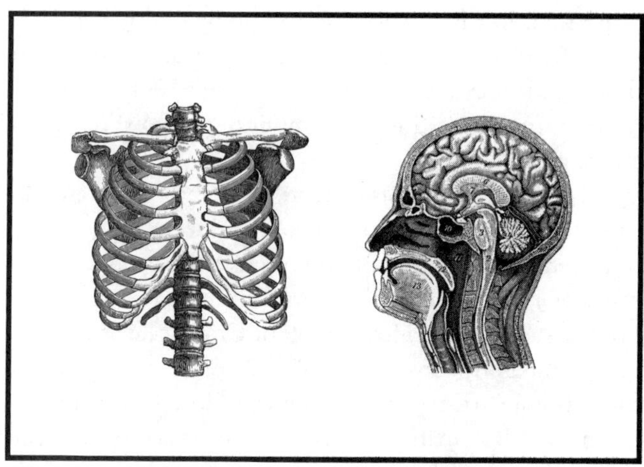

neither a ring for a finger nor a sword for its sheath are so well fitted as are the parts of the human body. What could better demonstrate the wisdom of the divine Artist than all these organs and instruments that He made with such perfection for the fulfillment of their functions?

It should be evident how ridiculous is the opinion which states that our bodies were made by chance. Things that are made by chance rarely turn out well, but a body composed of innumerable parts and organs, so perfectly constructed that it surpasses all created intelligence could not have come about by chance; it must be the work of a supreme intelligence. Would it not be the height of foolishness to say that on removing a mass of metal from a furnace, one could expect to find a perfectly fashioned watch, with all its wheels and parts in perfect balance? How much more foolish it is to state that the human body was fashioned by chance in the womb of the mother, when the bones and sinews and other parts of our body are much more numerous and more complicated than the parts of any watch?

This is why students of anatomy rightly maintain that this study is a certain and secure guide to lead us to a knowledge of the Creator and of His perfections or attributes as manifested in His creatures. Hence, the human body is sometimes called a book of God, because in every part of the body, however small, one can read and observe the supreme artistry and wisdom of God. In this microcosm, which is man, there is no vein or artery or bone, nothing so small that it does not proclaim the excellence and artistry of Him who made it.

What marvelous things the anatomists say of the human eye, the skeleton, and the remarkable network of the nervous system and brain! What a wonderful thing is the human hand, which has produced a vast artificial world wherein is to be found almost as much variety as in the world created directly by God! Consequently, I consider them fortunate indeed who dedicate themselves to the study of the structure of the human body, for if they but raise their minds to God and see the human body as the work of His hands, they will time and again be overwhelmed by the marvels and wonders that He has made.

David says in the Psalms that those who go down to the sea in ships see there the works of the Lord and His wonders in the deep (Psalm 106:23-24). This is no less true of those who enter into themselves and contemplate what the Creator has done in the human body, for they will see there how God has provided man with all the instruments and organs necessary for the preservation of life, and so perfectly that nothing is superfluous or lacking.

Nor is it any less a cause of admiration when we consider how these various organs and faculties are situated in the body. It is impossible to imagine another body more beautiful or better designed for the purposes for which it was created. The ancients said of the eloquence of Plato that if a wise man were to change a single word from one of his discourses, even after long consideration and thought, he would rob it of its elegance. If all the wise men of the world, desiring to refashion the smallest part or member of the human body, were to form it in another manner or put it in a different location in the body, they would not only destroy its use and function, but they would also destroy the grace and harmony of the human body as a whole.

Realizing that the human intellect is incapable of understanding the excellence and artistry of the divine mind, Solomon stated that just as man does not know the paths of the winds or how the human body is fashioned in the womb of the mother, so also it does not fathom the works of the Creator who has made all things. David states that all things past and future are present to God and that darkness and night are as light to Him. Then, speaking of the human body, he says: "For You possessed my reins; You protected me from my mother's womb. I will praise You, for You are fearfully magnified; wonderful are Your works and my soul knows quite well. My bone is not hidden from You, which You made in secret; and my substance in the lower parts of the earth. Your eyes did see my imperfect being, and in Your book all shall be written. Days shall be formed, and no one in them. But to me Your friends, O God, are made exceedingly honorable. Their principality is made exceedingly strengthened. I will number them, and they shall be multiplied above the sand." (Psalm 138:13-18).

In these words, the prophet declares the wonderful wisdom of God which shines forth in a singular manner in the construction of the human body. We should especially note the phrase, "You are fearfully magnified," because the word "fearfully" would seem more properly to denote God's justice than His wisdom. But after considering the profundity of God's wisdom, which is so clearly manifested in this work, and the greatness of the divine power which could make such a variety and perfection of members and organs from a simple substance, the Psalmist was so amazed and overawed by the majesty and greatness of God that he deliberately used the word "fearfully." It is similar to the reaction experienced by a man who stands on a high cliff and looks down into a chasm. He feels that he is gradually losing his balance and fears that he will fall, although he may be standing in a secure and safe place. So also, David was filled with fear when, considering the wondrous work that is the human body, he realized the grandeur of the Creator who fashioned it.

Yet, it is not surprising that a prophet, filled with the spirit of God, should marvel at this work of God and be moved to praise and honor Him for it. Rather, it is surprising that we should find the same reaction in a pagan philosopher. Galen, the prince of doctors, wrote eighteen books on the human body, and when he saw how the power and greatness of God is manifested therein, he said that his writings were a hymn of praise and thanksgiving composed to the honor and glory of God. It is not an honor, he says, in which we offer incense to Him or sacrifice a hundred cattle. Rather, it is an honor in which, through the knowledge of this wonderful work of His hands, we acknowledge the supreme wisdom which fashioned such things, the power which executed such things, and the goodness which deigned so liberally to provide creatures with all that was necessary. The same idea was expressed by the prophet Hosea: "For I desired mercy, and not sacrifice, and the knowledge of God more than holocausts" (Hosea 6:6).

There is another marvel that is no less wonderful than the foregoing. The philosophers teach that our soul comes to us from outside ourselves and is not educed from the matter of which our body is formed, as are the souls of brute animals. The human soul is a spiritual substance, like that of the angels, so it could not proceed from any material because there is no proportion between these two things. After saying this much, many of the philosophers tell us no more about the human soul. But what the philosophers fail to tell us, we learn from the Christian religion: God by His own power creates the human soul and infuses it into the body which was conceived in the womb of the mother.

Let us first cast our eyes over the entire created universe, considering the various continents of Asia, Europe, Africa, and America, and all the islands in the various oceans and the many lands wherein indigenous peoples dwell. Let us consider the vast number of women who are pregnant or who are yet to carry in their wombs the bodies of children as yet unborn. Then we shall realize that day and night God is creating human souls and infusing them into bodies. This will continue until the end of time and in all parts of the world, as it has been going on since the foundation of the world until now.

All these creations and infusions of human souls are caused directly by God and not through the instrumentality of the heavens or the ministration of angels. Yet, God does not on that account lose any peace and tranquility, nor is it a source of anxiety or solicitude to Him. What must be the wisdom of such a God who at the proper moment and in all parts of the world is continually infusing souls in the matter disposed by the parents in the womb of the mother? What must be His careful and delicate concern? And what must be the power of a God who creates such beautiful spiritual souls out of no pre-existing material, and yet in each soul the image of God shines forth in a spiritual manner?

10

MAN'S LOWER FACULTIES

It will be helpful to recall some general notions that will enable us to understand vegetative powers of the human soul. The human soul possesses three types of powers or faculties. The first are the vegetative powers, and their primary functions are nourishment and growth; the second are called sensitive powers, to which we attribute the properties of sensation and movement; and the third are intellectual or rational powers, which distinguish men from brute creation and make them like unto the angels.

These three types of powers or faculties were given to the human soul by the Creator. This is a great marvel, for although the human soul is a simple substance, it is of such a nature that it possesses powers that are common to angels, animals, and plants and, consequently, it exercises

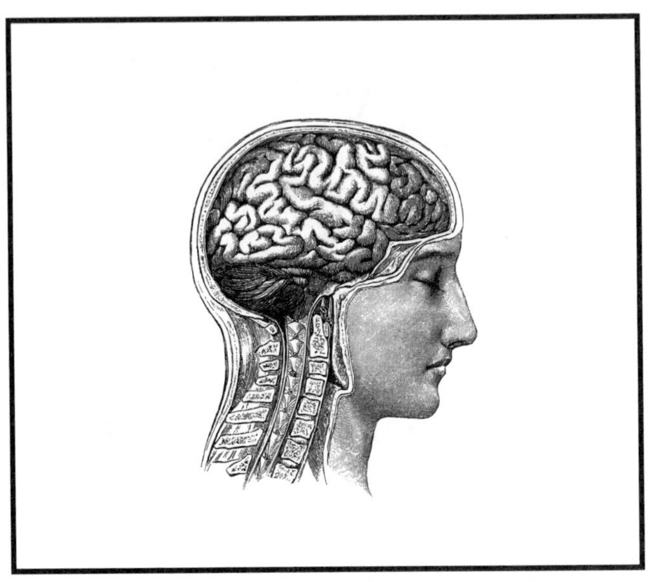

functions that are characteristic of these widely divergent beings. Consequently, man has the power of reason, as do the angels, but he also eats and reproduces like the brute animals.

We know that nourishment is necessary to maintain life. The reason for this is the natural heat of our bodies, which is the cause both of our death and of our life. The natural heat of the body gradually consumes the moisture and tissues of the body, so that they must be restored from time to time by the food that we eat. But since that which is restored is not as perfect as that which has been lost, the body one day reaches a point where it begins to lose its vigor, and ultimately life itself begins to wane, unless some disease or violence sets in to take life away earlier.

Now, since the entire body and all its parts need nourishment and repair, it has a system of channels or pathways throughout the body that carry nourishment and energy to the parts where they are needed. Thus, the Creator equipped the human body with veins and arteries. A similar phenomenon can be seen in the leaf of a tree, especially in larger leaves, where we see a network of veins, some large and others as fine as a hair, by which the leaf is nourished and preserved.

The Creator has also endowed the vegetative soul with three powers that are necessary for its maintenance: attraction, conversion, and expulsion. Each member of the body draws from the veins whatever is necessary for its nutrition and converts this into its own substance, and if there is anything superfluous, it is expelled. But the most amazing of these three powers is the power of attraction. The blood that circulates through the veins contains certain elements or humors that are beneficial to certain parts of the body. Each organ and member of the body selects from the blood whatever is suitable to its nature but does not touch the rest.[1]

If a magnet is surrounded by various metals, it will draw only the iron and leave the rest. A similar power

[1] Editor's note: In the 16th century when Ven. Louis wrote, elements such as oxygen had not been discovered and named, and he relies heavily on the writings Galen (see last note) and the findings of the medical schools of the day. Just the same, our modern understanding of circulation only strengthens the argument.

is found in the various organs of the body so that they select from the blood only that which is most suitable. We see the same thing verified by the animals. If you were to set out a piece of meat, some grains of wheat, and some green leaves, a sheep would eat the greens, a dog would eat the meat, and a hen would eat the grain. He that gave the animals an instinctive knowledge of their proper food, also gave to the members and organs of the human body the power to abstract from the blood whatever nourishment they need.

The human body also manifests a remarkable harmony, because all the members of the body complement and serve each other, and at the same time that they perform their functions for the common good of the whole body. Thus, the lower members and organs serve the higher, and these, in turn, make use of and govern the functions of the lesser faculties. Moreover, God does not wish anything to be lost or useless. For that reason, He has so fashioned the human body that whatever is excessive or superfluous in one part may be of service in another part, as we see in the case of the bile, which is distilled by the liver and is then used for the nourishment of the spleen.

In addition, the Author of nature fashions the proper instrument for each office or function. In the house of a moderately rich man only one or two servants do all the work of the house. But in the palace of a king there are a great number of offices and officials, each one deputed to a certain duty. Applying this example to the case at hand, there has never been any royal house or palace in the whole world that possessed as many servants as does the royal house of our body, which was fashioned by God as a dwelling place for our soul. However numerous and varied the offices and functions of the body, there is no member or organ that has more than one function, and if any appears to have more than one duty, it is by reason of the diversity of parts that are in it. We see this not only from the five external senses but even more so from the internal members of the body, such as the stomach, the intestines, the liver, the heart, and so forth. Not only does this manifest the marvelous order of divine providence, but it also serves to give instruction and knowledge in the field of medicine. For if doctors understand the nature and functions of the various parts of the body and their intimate relationship and interdependence, they can learn how to apply medicines and treatments for regaining or preserving the health of the body.

The nature and functions of the human body should demonstrate how smoothly divine providence arranges and disposes all things, proceeding from causes to effects and disposing those causes in proportion to the excellence of the effects to be produced. The more noble the form that He desires to introduce, the more perfectly He disposes the matter in which that form is to be received, for there must be no disproportion between cause and effect and matter and form. Applying this principle to spiritual matters, we can understand that it is necessary for us to dispose ourselves properly for any given degree of grace. Accordingly, the penitent sinner who desires to reap the fruit and benefit of a good confession will make a good examination of conscience, will be filled with sorrow and repentance for his past sins, and will have a firm purpose of amendment. Likewise, to receive the fruits of the Holy Eucharist, one will strive not only to be free from sin but also to have actual devotion, rejecting all thoughts and distractions that may lessen that devotion. Indeed, for any grace or spiritual gift one must make the proper preparations and be properly disposed to receive them.

Accordingly, he who desires to enjoy the sweetness and consolation of the Holy Spirit must rid himself of all the tastes and consolations of the world, as David did, when he said: "My soul refused to be comforted; I remembered God and was delighted" (Psalm 76:4). Likewise, he who would aspire to the perfection of the love of God must detach himself from the disordered love of worldly things. If he would seek to be so united with God as to be one spirit with Him, which is to become a spiritual and divine man, he must mortify whatever is earthly and carnal in him and may prove an impediment to the divine. If he desires to be like unto God, who is his one and highest good, he must withdraw from things of the world, even from those things that are not in themselves evil, for although they be good in themselves, they may easily demand too much of his attention and smother his spirit of devotion.

Further, if in his pursuit of spiritual things, a man desires to give himself to the contemplative life and wishes also to have a mind that is tranquil and free of other considerations when he thinks about God, he must be, as the saints advise, deaf, blind, and mute to the things of the world. If he acts otherwise, he can only be disturbed by worldly thoughts and distractions. Finally, he who desires to find God should realize that he must truly seek Him, and he who wishes to attain the greatest gifts must conform his work and efforts to the dignity of those gifts, just as one who desires to be learned must be diligent in study.

Solomon teaches us this truth when he tells us that if we wish to possess true wisdom, we should seek it as arduously as men work for money and as zealously as men dig for treasures in the earth (Proverbs 2:4). Moses also states that we shall find God if we seek Him with our whole heart and with all the energy of our being (Deuteronomy 4:29). This is the ordinary manner in which our Lord communicates His gifts and graces to His creatures: He first disposes them and prepares them to receive such gifts. It is true, however, that God is not restricted by the laws according to which He normally and commonly operates, for without any previous disposition or preparation and as a sign of His liberality and magnificence, He sometimes bestows unexpected gifts, as we see in the conversion of St. Paul and the vocations of St. Peter, St. James, and St. John, who were called to the dignity of apostles as they mended their nets.

11

THE LIFE OF THE SENSES

The human soul, although one and simple, possesses the characteristics and properties of the three different kinds of soul. Consequently, the one and the same soul is the principle of the operations of man's lower faculties and organs, of his sensations and movements, and also of the operations of his intellect and will.

In our sensitive life, which we share with the animals, divine wisdom shines forth even more resplendently in this higher activity of the soul because the sensitive operations are more noble than those of the vegetative level.

Since all our knowledge comes to us through the external senses, which are concerned with material things, and since we cannot see or touch or taste spiritual things, many men either do not believe in the existence of spiritual realities or do not understand the power and virtue that they possess. Such was the case with the Sadducees, who were so dull intellectually that they did not believe in angels or spiritual beings. There are also other men today who, although they accept the existence of such beings on faith, cannot understand how such things can exist without bodies. So, they do not appreciate or understand the dignity, excellency, and power of their own souls, since they imagine the soul as some sort of airy substance. I should like to take such men by the hand and lead them little by little to a realization of the dignity and power of spiritual beings so that they would arrive at a better understanding of the nature and power of their own spiritual souls.

From looking at nature it should be evident that the more gross and earthly a thing is, the less power and efficacy it possesses, whereas the more immaterial and spiritual, the more noble and powerful it is. In this way we can understand something of the dignity of our human soul, which is a purely spiritual substance, as are the angels. And since the human soul is a spiritual substance, we should not be surprised to see the variety of offices and functions that it performs. What God works in the greater universe or macrocosm, our human soul effects in this smaller universe or microcosm.

We have said that the sensitive soul is not only the principle of movement but also of sensation, so we turn to man's external and internal senses. The external senses are five in number and they are united, so to speak, in

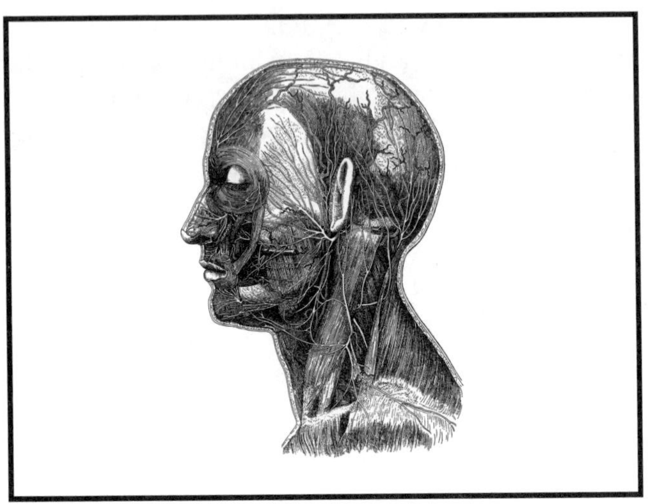

an internal sense which is called the common sense. The nerves that proceed from the brain to the end organs of the various external senses give sensibility to these receptors. Likewise, the species and images of things perceived by the outer senses are carried to the brain along the same nerve track. The common sense then enables us to perceive the various images and sensations as a pattern or unity. This is the beginning of our knowledge, for there is nothing in the intellect which was not first presented in some way to the senses.

A second internal sense, the imagination, receives the sense images and preserves them faithfully. Like the common sense, it is also located in the brain. A third power or internal sense is called the estimative power or instinct in animals, but in men it is called the cogitative power. This faculty is the most spiritual of all the internal senses and enables us to perceive things that have neither form nor body. Thus, a sheep perceives an enemy in the wolf but sees the dog as a friend. Although such concepts have no material counterpart, the Creator provides both men and animals with an instinctive power for discerning between those things that are beneficial and those that are dangerous and harmful.

The fourth internal sense, also localized in the brain, is the power of memory. This faculty enables us to recall past events as past, and if the memory is strong, it is a great help in acquiring the virtue of prudence, which relies to a great extent on the recollection of past experiences. Memory is also the mother of eloquence and it helps us in all the arts and sciences by enabling us to remember rules and precepts without which, as they say, reading books or attending lectures would be like pouring water into a sieve. Lastly, memory makes us grateful to God by recalling the many favors received from Him.

Now we move to the external senses. David was right in confessing that God is admirable in all His works, however small, and what is more admirable than the eye! Professors and students in such matters confess that the human eye is the most delicate and remarkable organ that God has fashioned in the human body and that it is no less beneficial than it is marvelous. What is more pitiful than a man without sight? The saintly Tobias, who so patiently endured the loss of his eyesight, was greeted by the angel with the hope that God would give joy to him. And Tobias answered: "What manner of joy shall be to me, who sit in darkness and see not the light of heaven?" (Tobit 5:12)

Our admiration is aroused first of all by the species and images that are required in order that we may see external objects. All visible things have color and, consequently, they are able to produce images and likenesses of themselves, which in philosophy we call a species and which represent things as they really are. The necessity for such species, as the philosophers state, arises from the fact that in order to produce a certain effect, a cause must be in contact, substantially or virtually, with the thing on which it is to act. But the various external objects that we wish to see are at some distance from the eye. Somehow, the objects of vision must come into contact with the human eye. To bring this about, the Creator has provided that the images or species of external objects should be conveyed to the eye through the medium of light.

The human eye then receives these impressions like a mirror, and since the eye is not transparent, the light waves cannot pass through. As a result, the eye faithfully represents whatever is placed before it. Thus, the eye can see mountains, valleys, fields, trees, entire armies, and anything else that is in front of it, and if thousands of eyes were fixed on the same object, all would reflect that same object. This is true not only of the things nearby, but also of things in the heavens. For we could not see the stars which are so far removed from us if their likeness were not impressed on our eyes to serve as a medium of vision.

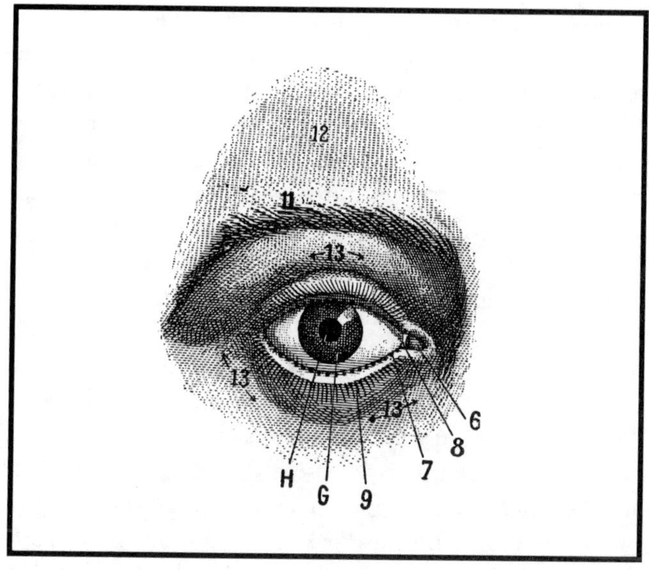

The eyeball is made up of three layers. The first is an opaque and tough layer that gives form to the eyeball and covers it entirely, except for a small area in front where the layer is transparent and crystalline. The second layer or tunic is reddish brown in color and contains a network of blood vessels. It terminates at the iris of the eye, which serves as a colored diaphragm and regulates the amount of light that enters the eye. The third and deepest layer is the retina and it contains the nerve endings for actual vision. Passing through these various layers, the representations of external objects are ultimately carried along the nerve track to the common sense, which is located in the brain.

Consequently, we can say that the whole visible creation enters our soul through the portals of the eyes. That is the reason why Aristotle states that the sense of sight is so precious: man, as a rational animal, naturally desires to know things, and it is the sense of sight that reveals to him the infinite variety of things in the visible universe. God has given us a most precious gift!

More excellent still is the fact that through vision we can see the marvels of the works of God which raises our soul to a knowledge of Him. David says: "I will behold Your heavens, O Lord, the works of Your fingers; the moon and the stars which You have founded" (Psalm 8:4). This saintly king used the sense of sight in a much better manner than do those who use it to offend God, making an instrument of sin that which has been given for God's praise and glory, and thus making war on the Giver with the very gift He gave them. What a remarkable gift is that of sight! If you were to lose your sight, what would you do? Where would you go to find a remedy? And what thanks you would give to one who could restore your sight!

The sense of hearing is also a noble sense and no less helpful in acquiring wisdom. The inner ear is connected by a nerve tract to the brain and the common sense, which is the ultimate terminus of sensations. Separating the inner and outer ear is a delicate membrane like the covering of a drum, and as the vibrations of air move this membrane, sound is transmitted to the inner ear and ultimately to the brain. But if this drum or membrane should be punctured

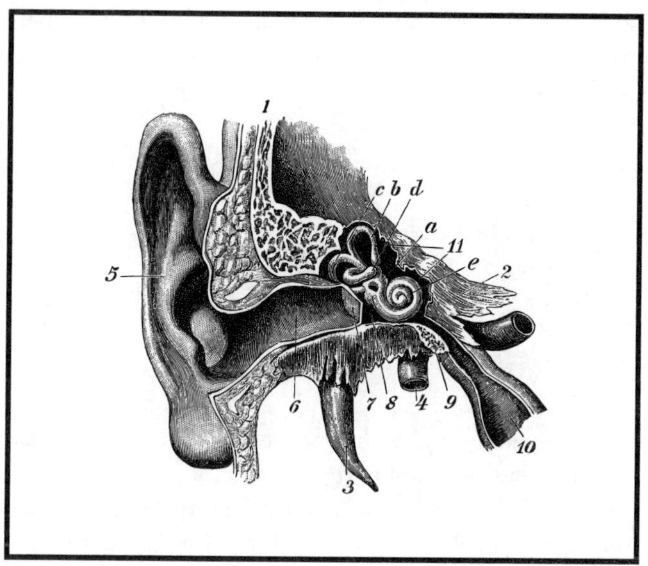

or broken through injury, hearing is destroyed. For that reason, the Creator has provided the outer ear to protect this membrane, just as He has supplied the eyelid to protect the eye.

The sense of smell is also connected with the common sense and the brain by means of a nerve track. The nerve endings terminate in the soft and delicate mucous membrane of the nostrils where the particles of external objects come into contact with the membrane and cause a sensation. To protect the sense of smell, the Creator has provided the nose, which also serves to beautify the face. Here again we see the infinite wisdom of God who knew how to join in the structure of our senses and members two qualities that are united only with great difficulty: utility and beauty.

Then comes the sense of taste, whereby we can enjoy the flavor of food. The sensation of taste is caused by the fact that the tongue is humid, filled with pores, and of itself lacks any kind of taste. The tongue is filled with pores so that the particles of food may come in contact with the nerve endings or taste buds that receive the sensation. The tongue is humid so that the food may be saturated with saliva. Otherwise the nerve endings in the pores of the tongue would not come in contact with the food and there would be no sensation. It is no less necessary that the tongue has no taste of its own, just as the ear of itself is void of sound, otherwise the tongue could not distinguish between various tastes. For if the tongue had its own flavor, it would experience this taste and no other, as happens in the case of the sick or feverish to whom all things taste bitter or insipid because of the phlegmatic condition of the patient.

The last external sense is that of touch, whereby we receive sensations of the qualities of bodies, such as cold and heat, humidity and dryness, solidity, resistance, and pressure, as well as roughness, smoothness, and softness. This sense is not localized in any specific organ but it extends over the entire body, so that men and animals can be aware of what is helpful or harmful and may flee the one and seek the other.

To conclude this subject, I should like to summarize what the Roman philosopher Cicero says concerning the utility and beauty of the external senses and various parts of the human body. He begins his account by stating that divine providence raised up men from the earth and made them to walk and stand upright, so that by looking at the heavens they could come to a knowledge of God. For men are not made to be permanent inhabitants of this earth, but to contemplate heavenly and sovereign things, and this is given to no other animal but man.

Divine providence has marvelously fashioned the external senses, which serve as the interpreters and messengers of external things and has localized them in the head of man as in a lofty tower. Since the eyes serve as watchtowers of the body, they have been placed in the highest part, so that they may better exercise their office. The ears were fashioned for the perception of sound and for that reason they also have been fittingly placed at the upper part of man's body. For a similar reason, the sense of smell is located in the head, because vapors naturally tend upward and carry with them the particles of odor. The sense of smell was wisely placed near the mouth, because the odor of things that we eat and drink plays an important role in judging whether a thing is good or bad. The sense of taste must differentiate between various things by which we are nourished and for that reason it is rightly located in the mouth, through which pass the things that we eat and drink. Lastly, the sense of touch is rightly extended throughout the whole body so that we may be aware of wounds and blows, cold and heat, or anything that may do us harm.

Since wise men usually give more protection to things that are precious than to those that are base or common, the divine Artist has placed greater safeguards around the eyes than around the other senses, for the eyes are much more valuable and more highly esteemed. He first covered them with very delicate layers of skin that are transparent at the front so that we may see through them, but He also made them of a tough and durable matter so that they would stand much use. He has fashioned the eyes so that they could be easily moved from side to side, in order that a man may quickly turn away from anything harmful or easily cast his glance on what he desires to see. The pupil of the eye is relatively small, to give sharpness of vision and to lessen the danger of harm to vision. The lids of the eye are soft and flexible so that they will not irritate the eye itself, but at the same time they can be opened and closed with the greatest ease to prevent anything harmful from entering the eye. The eyelids are furnished with lashes, which are like little brushes, so that when the eyes are opened, they can catch whatever shall fall upon them. Moreover, the eyes are set more deeply into the head and above them are the eyebrows, which also serve as a protection, as when they prevent perspiration from the forehead from running into the eyes. Beneath the eyes the fleshy cheeks likewise serve as a protection and form the valley in which the eyes are set. Finally, the nose protrudes from between the eyes and thus serves as a fence or wall to protect them.

The ears are always open, because we have need of hearing even while we are asleep, so that we can be awakened by a sound. The canal of the ear has many twists and turns, for if it were short and straight, something harmful could easily enter in. But if an insect or anything noxious should enter into the canal of the ear, it is caught in the natural wax that serves as a snare. The outer ear or pinna protects the auditory canal and also helps to convey sounds to the inner ear. The flesh around the entrance of the outer ear is hard and trumpet-shaped so that the sound waves will more easily be received and even magnified when necessary.

The nose also is always open, in order to fulfill its proper function, and it has two narrow entrances so that harmful objects from outside cannot easily enter it. It is also supplied with a mucous-like substance and discharge so that dust and other particles can easily be expelled.[1] On the other hand, the sense of taste is very carefully enclosed within the mouth, so that it can the better perform its office and also be protected.

These observations from the writings of Cicero manifest to us the supreme wisdom and counsel with which God has fashioned and protected all the external senses. He has not neglected a single detail, however small. How much more care must He exert over the great things in creation if He is so particular about the lesser things?

---

[1] Editor's note: The mucous in the nose also stops harmful bacteria from entering. However, bacteria had not been discovered at that time.

12

THE PASSIONS

Since we have spoken of the internal and external senses, we now turn to the affective part of the sensitive soul, where the passions and emotions are located. Since they enable man to desire and seek beneficial things and to flee harmful things, they are necessary for our conservation.

Among the passions are two principal ones that are, so to speak, the root and foundation of all the others: love for particular goods that are beneficial to us and hatred of those things that are harmful to us. Thus, the animal seeks what is good and convenient for its conservation and avoids the evil that would work for its destruction. Without these two basic passions, the animal would be like a bird without wings, for it would not then be able to seek its good or to avoid the opposite.

Moreover, all the other passions spring from the two basic passions of love and hatred. When the good that we love is absent, desire springs forth, but when the good is actually possessed, we experience joy. On the other hand, from the hatred of an absent evil springs aversion or flight, but when the evil is present to us, we experience sorrow. These six passions, love, desire, joy, hate, aversion, and sorrow, are called the concupiscible appetites, because their function is to seek and desire sensible goods.

However, if the good to which we are drawn by love is difficult but possible to obtain, the desire we have for it is accompanied by the hope of attaining it, for men readily hope for the things that they desire. But if the difficulties or obstacles to the desired good are so great as to be insuperable, then they kill our hope, and the contrary passion of despair is aroused. At other times, if our desire for a good is very intense and we judge that we can successfully extricate ourselves from a dangerous situation, courage is aroused to face the threatening evil. But if the difficulties and obstacles are so great as to be insuperable in the face of danger or evil, the passion of fear is aroused. This passion serves as a protection for the animal, so that it will not attempt to do that which it cannot, but will seek another remedy, such as flight or hiding. But if, in addition to this, one finds himself completely impeded from the attainment of what he desires or if he loses the good that he once possessed, he then bristles with anger, which is the avenger of the hurts and disappointments that we suffer.

These five irascible passions are also necessary preserve

our life. If we possessed appetites merely for the things that are suitable for our preservation, but had no courage or valor for overcoming the difficulties that often accompany them, we would never attain many of them and we would, therefore, lack many things that are necessary for life. But the divine Governor, who has been deficient in nothing, took care to provide us with the five passions of hope, despair, courage, fear, and anger. Each in its own way helps us overcome the difficulties that beset us or warns us to fear danger and not to hope for victory when it is impossible.

We find here an application that is very profitable for the spiritual life. From what has been said of the various passions and their function in human life, those who have ardent desires for perfection will understand that good desires are not enough to obtain the virtues that they seek. Desires must be accompanied by great courage and fortitude in overcoming the difficulties that inevitably beset the good Christian in his pursuit of virtue. Consequently, if we expend no valor or effort in the acquisition and increase of virtue, a man will remain sterile and without fruit, in spite of all his good desires. Hence the saying that hell is paved with good intentions but paradise is filled with good works. However, when the desire for virtue is intense, it is usually accompanied by valor and courage.

The passions not only serve for the preservation of human life and of the human species, but they also assist greatly in the practice of certain virtues. Thus, anger is the instigator of vindictive justice, which has as its function the punishment of the criminal. Because of the anger and indignation felt toward such persons, judges are moved to punish them. So, Aristotle has wisely said that anger is good for a soldier, but not for a captain.

Likewise, from the desire for those things we judge to be good, two affections spring. If they are well regulated, they will be of great help in acquiring virtue and avoiding vice. These are namely: love of honor and a sense of shame. Since noble men and rulers generally have a high regard for honor, the divine Governor has made virtue honorable, so that men would esteem virtue. It is as if He had sweetened virtue and placed honor as a bait to make men seek it, although it would not be a true virtue if sought only for this reason. Such was the basis of the heroic deeds of the Romans, who attempted heroic feats in the name of honor. For the same reason, Scipio and the other Roman captains did not accept the beautiful maidens that were presented to them, but returned them to their husbands or fathers.

As the love of honor attracts the heart to virtue, so also does the sense of shame withdraw men from vice, because of the disgrace and dishonor that follow in its wake. God has especially imprinted a sense of shame in the hearts of women, to serve as a bulwark of chastity. It is fitting that the wisest Creator should provide greater protection for that which is more precious and more ardently desired. So, in addition to the virginal seal, He has given women this natural sense of shame, which acts as a rein upon the vice of impurity.

The passions are of themselves neither virtuous nor vicious, but are natural inclinations which may be good or evil according to the use we make of them. When the passions, which are in the lower part of the soul, follow the dictates of the superior part, where the intellect and will are located, they can be used well and for the purposes for which they were given to us. But when they follow a rule other than reason, as when they are moved by the imagination or the apprehension of sensible things, they lose their way, because they follow a blind leader.

The hierarchy of our spiritual kingdom is so arranged that the will is like a king that commands all the members and faculties of man, and the intellect is the faithful counselor of the will. It makes known to the will the dignity and excellence of spiritual things so that the will can love them, and it points out the ugliness of sin and vice so that the will can abhor them. The will has as its servants, the bodily organs, which are moved in conformity with the command of the will and without any resistance. They obey as they are commanded. But there are also in this kingdom, as in all kingdoms, fawns or parasites that advise the king to do things that are improper. Such is the role of the passions when they attach themselves to sensible and delightful goods and seek to draw the king to the same sensate things, although the intellect objects and warns the king that such goods are dangerous. And when the passions are strong enough to blind the intellect and pervert the will, they take the reins into their own hands. We have an example of this in a person suffering from intense thirst. He knows how much damage drinking will do to him, but the desire for water is so intense that it carries the will with it and the man drinks his fill.

The evil effects of original sin are most in evidence in our passions and appetites. As long as Adam and Eve were in the state of innocence, all their appetites were under control, well regulated, and obedient to reason. But once the gift of original justice had been lost by sin, the passions were let loose to rebel against reason. As a consequence, the world and the devil wage a relentless war against us through the passions.

By reason of the appetites and passions our flesh is naturally inclined and attracted to the things that are in conformity with its nature. The enemy takes advantage of this by arousing the passions and putting them in disorder so that they will exceed the limits and control of reason. Thus, Job says of the devil that he fans the flames by his breathing, that is, he blows on the flames of our passions so that they pass beyond the limits of temperance.

In the beginning, man committed sin through the instigation of the woman; the stronger yielded to the weaker. Now the devil generally wages war against us in our weakest part, that part which is naturally inclined to the things of earth. The devil has this to his advantage: that the weaker and baser part of our nature inclines us to the very things that he desires of us. In this way, he inflames these desires and inclinations by means of his suggestions, with the result that the passions, which could have been beneficial to us if rightly used and controlled, easily become a source of ruin and corruption. Hence arises the disordered love for honor from which ambition springs, the desire for money from which avarice springs, the longing for sensual delights which is the source of gluttony and other intemperate acts, the hatred and unrestrained anger against those who try to keep us from the enjoyment of sensate goods, the envy of those who possess things that we desire for ourselves, and every other kind of vice.

We can see that just as the defenders of a besieged city put all their strength and resistance at the weakest point, where the enemies are trying to make a breach in order to enter, so the true servant of God should understand that the Christian life is a perpetual battle and constant warfare. And since life is one long struggle and temptation, the profession of the Christian is to be a man of war. As a soldier constantly under siege, he will protect and defend this weakest point of his passions so that he will not be overcome.

13

GOD'S IMAGE AND LIKENESS

The highest part of the soul is the intellectual and rational part. Man's rational soul is spiritual, like the angelic substance, and for that reason it is not localized in any bodily member or organ, as are the internal and external senses. It is, therefore, the rational soul that distinguishes us from brute creation and makes us like unto God and the angels. The Creator Himself testifies to this when at the creation of man when He said: "Let Us make man to Our image and likeness."

With what solemnity the Creator proceeded to the creation of man! In fashioning other creatures, He did nothing more than say: "Let it be made," and immediately it was made. But in the creation of man He used a different formula and statement, for He said: "Let Us make." This signifies that the three Persons of the Trinity were immediately concerned with the creation of God's noblest creature in this visible universe.

God said: "Let Us make man to Our image and likeness." To be an image of God pertains only to men and angels. All other creatures, even the sun and moon and stars, are not called images of God, but vestiges or traces of God. Since men and angels manifest much more of the grandeur of the Creator, they are called images of God.

When God, as Scripture tells us, had formed man's body out of the slime of the earth, He breathed into this body the spark of life. And since the breath proceeds from the interior of the one who breathes, God wished by this act to have us know that the soul is something that proceeds from the bosom of God Himself. It is not part of the divine substance, as some heretics taught, but in many ways, it shares in the attributes of God, as we shall soon see.

One of the aspects of the soul that has aroused the admiration of all wise men and especially manifests the divine power is the diversity of its functions. The human soul is at once purely spiritual and the form of the material body to which it gives life. But there is such a great discrepancy between purely spiritual things and material things that the disproportion between them does not permit them to be easily blended and united. Therefore, it must be taken as one of God's great wonders that He could impart such power and efficacy to the human soul that it can understand lofty and immaterial things as does the angel and that it also enables men to reproduce themselves as do the animals. It is as if God had made a creature that is part angel and part animal, for in man we find the powers proper to each of these vastly different creatures. With good reason could St. Augustine say that of all God's marvelous works the greatest is the creation of man.

Let us examine the various reasons why man is said to be an image of God. If we understand this, we shall also grasp something of man's dignity and we shall realize more fully the debt of gratitude we owe to God for the many blessings we have received from Him. Moreover, the man who appreciates his dignity will be less inclined to disfigure the divine image by debasing himself with the things of the flesh.

In the first place, man is said to be an image of God by reason of the intellect and free will that he possesses, as do God and the angels. None of the creatures inferior to man possess the prerogative of liberty, for they are all natural agents that cannot cease to do that for which they have been given the faculties and powers. But man is free and is master of his deeds; he can do or not do as he wishes.

But it is not only man's freedom and liberty that distinguish him from animal creation. He is also an image of God by reason of his intellect, for God is also an intellectual substance, though in a much more eminent degree than is man. Man's likeness to God on the part of his intellect is especially evident in the works of art that he produces. It is said that art imitates nature as far as it can, but this is merely another way of saying that man imitates God in his manner of working.

The Author of nature has fashioned the teeth to cut and to chew food, the hands to work, the feet to walk, and the framework of the skeleton to bear the weight of the body. Man observes the same rule in the production of the works of art, as we see in the cutting of the cloth for his clothing, the shoes that he makes to fit his feet, the house that he constructs as his dwelling place, and the ships that he builds for navigation. Each product is proportioned to the end for which it has been made.

We have already mentioned that the Creator takes care to combine utility with beauty in the works of His hands, as is evident in the human countenance with its nose, eyes, eyelids, and lashes. All these serve to beautify the human face at the same time that they perform the various functions that each was meant to fulfill, and if any of them were changed, the beauty and utility of the face would also be lessened. So also, in the production of the works of art, man imitates God to the best of his ability by trying to make artificial things both useful and beautiful. Visit the homes of the wealthy and you will find that the furnishings of these homes are constructed to serve not only for utility but also for beauty and adornment. Walk through the streets of any large city and you will see that the numerous offices and buildings or the variety of ships and boats in its port serve the same double purpose. And if you were to end your tour by entering a church or cathedral, you would discover the beauty of religious art in the architecture of the building, the ornamentation of the altars, and the inspiring melodies of the chant that fills the church with God's praise.

If you were to visit a country fair or city market, you would again find countless products of man's ingenuity and art that compete with the art and genius of nature herself, not only as to construction and beauty but also as to the variety of things made. God created the world and filled it with a wide diversity of creatures. Human art, in imitation of God, has made another world of artificial things.

It is also a singular perfection of God that He is present in all places, in the world and above and beyond the world. In its own way, our rational soul can also go to all parts of the world whenever it wishes. Although we may now be in Italy, says St. Ambrose, we can think of the things of the East and West. We can unite ourselves mentally with people of Persia or Africa, and we can travel in spirit with those who travel. We can be present to those who are absent, and we can even resurrect the dead, as it were, and speak with them as if they were living. We are to understand by this that it is not the bodily part of us that is made in God's likeness, but that part of us which enables us to see those who are absent, to travel across the ocean, to scrutinize what is hidden, to view all the parts of the world, to descend into hell or to rise to heaven, and even to be joined with Christ.

A still greater proof that our souls are made to the image and likeness of God is the fact that the human soul, in addition to being a spiritual substance, is the principle and cause of all the functions performed by the body wherein it dwells. God works in all the creatures of this vast universe, conserving them in being and giving them the power to perform the functions for which He made them.

In like manner, our soul has full power and authority over the body and its functions, so that the human body performs no operation of which the soul is not in some way the principle and origin and cause. This is evident from the fact that a dead person ceases entirely to operate because the soul is separated from the body.

As a simple and spiritual substance, the soul is the

principle of all the functions and operations of life. It is the soul that sees through the eyes, hears through the ears, smells, tastes, and touches, digests food in the stomach, converts nourishment into blood and disperses it through the network of veins and arteries, and supplies energy to the nervous system throughout the body. The soul likewise paints the pictures that are found in the imagination, retains the millions of things in the memory, discusses and argues with the intellect, and loves or hates with the will. Nothing is so small or insignificant in our body that it does not have the soul as its cause and principle. But if the soul is removed from the body, all the functions and operations of the body cease.

David shows how astonished he was at this when he said: "Your knowledge is become wonderful to me; it is high, and I cannot reach it" (Psalm 138[139]:6). Theodoret of Cyrus declares, in his commentary on this verse: "O Lord, when recollected in spirit and freed from the cares of the world and external affairs, I enter into myself and contemplate my own nature, and especially the rational soul that You gave me, I might consider the knowledge of which it is capable and the arts invented by it to make life more pleasant and easy."

Or again, I might see how this soul governs the entire body, how it entrusts to the eyes the office of distinguishing between colors, to the tongue the distinction of tastes and the transmission of concepts by words, to the nose the perception of odors, to the ears the discernment of sounds, and to the sense of touch the awareness of pain or pleasure. Now, when I consider all these things and see how they concur in the general structure of man, with his remarkable blending of the mortal and the immortal, I am astonished at so great a miracle. And since the human mind cannot fathom anything so wonderful, I confess that I am overcome and am forced to break out into hymns of praise and to exclaim with the prophet: "Your knowledge is become wonderful to me; it is high, and I cannot reach it."

But what is meant by the statement that man is made not only in the image of God but also in His likeness? To this St. Bernard and St. Augustine respond by saying that the soul is called an image of God in regard to all that it has received according to its nature and it is called a likeness of God in regard to that which it has received gratuitously. They mean that the soul is an image of God in respect to the faculties and powers of the natural order that were bestowed upon it for the exercises of the natural life that is proper to it. It is called the likeness of God by reason of the supernatural graces and virtues that were showered on it by God so that it could live the supernatural life and merit eternal life.

It would follow from this that the soul's image of God, based as it is on the natural order, can never be lost, although the soul itself be condemned to hell. But the soul's likeness to God is destroyed whenever the soul loses sanctifying grace through any mortal sin. It is a terrible calamity for a man to experience the loss of this divine likeness and to be inflicted with the likeness that takes its place. As the Psalmist tells us: "And man, when he was in honor, did not understand; he is compared to senseless beasts and is become like to them" (Psalm 48:13). What is more lamentable than the horrible fall whereby man, who in the purity of his life bore the likeness of God, exchanges the divine likeness for that of the beasts? How much lower could human misery fall and to what greater depths could it descend? One can see from this how great is the malice of sin, which has caused such a grave misfortune.

Consider also that while the Creator is infinite in every way, the human soul is infinite in its capacity, its duration, its understanding, and its wisdom. It is infinite in capacity because there is nothing that it cannot comprehend, except God Himself. It is infinite in duration because it is immortal and will live forever, as long as God is God. It is infinite in its ability to understand and in its wisdom, because it could never understand or comprehend so many things that there would not yet remain something for it to know, something yet to discover. And even after a man would have understood all the arts and sciences of which human ingenuity is capable, his intellectual powers would still not be exhausted, but could know infinitely more than had already been known. Hence, the potentiality of the human intellect knows neither limit nor end, for a man can never learn so much that he cannot learn more.

O God, if all the causes and motives for love are summarized and centered in You to an eminent degree, why do I not love You with the full capacity of my love? If we were to see any one of these motives of love in any creature, we would love that creature with such abandon that we would gladly die for it. Why, then, Lord, are we not inflamed with Your love? Why do we not melt with love and desire to suffer a thousand deaths for love of You? If we recall the benefits we have received from You, we shall realize that we owe You the greatest debt of gratitude. If we consider love itself, we shall see that no one loves us more than You. Who is more perfect than You, more good, more beautiful, more kind, more noble, more wise, more powerful, and more generous?

What is it, Lord, that prevents our hearts from running to You? What bonds could be so strong that they hold us captive and prevent us from reaching You? If it is a love for the things of this world, how can such fragile and passing things hold back the impetus of our love for You? Will a little blade of grass be sufficient to resist a stone that comes hurtling down a mountain side?

Some may say that although all the motives and causes of love are centered in You, there is no proportion between something so lowly as ourselves and something so lofty as You. You are most excellent; man is most base. You are a spirit inaccessible and incomprehensible; man is flesh, miserable flesh. But to whom could my soul bear greater likeness than to You, Lord, since I have been made in Your image? To whom is my heart better proportioned than to You, since You created it for Yourself? My soul was made to be a vessel of election so that You could fill it with Yourself and no created thing could ever fill it completely. You are a spirit and our souls are spiritual; You are invisible and our souls are invisible; You are immortal and our souls are immortal; You possess an intellect and free will and our souls possess these qualities also. You are perfect goodness and holiness and power; if the devil does not erase the likeness we bear to You, our souls are likewise filled with virtue and goodness.

May Your name be ever blessed for making us like unto Yourself and for making us for Yourself. So truly are we made for each other that we can exclaim with the spouse in the Canticle: "My Beloved to me, and I to Him." The fact that You are so lofty and we so lowly increases the motives for love. Much more lovable is the likeness that is accompanied by inequality than that which is in every way equal. Greater is the love of the father for his son and the wife for her husband than the love between brothers, who are equal in all things. More sweet is the harmony of two different voices blending in the one melody, than when both voices sing on the same note. Therefore, although there is a kind of likeness and equality between Yourself and us, the disproportion between us is a cause of greater love. When a thing is imperfect, it inclines to a greater love of the perfect so that it may partake of greater perfection. So it is, Lord, that in our lowliness we do not lose sight of You. In Your light we see You as the true light, and although You are most powerful, You are no less good than You are great. Your greatness and power make You supreme, but Your goodness makes You merciful so as not to despise men.

But the reason why we do not love You as much as You should be loved is because of that first sin, through which human nature was so inclined to itself that it tends to love all things for itself and direct everything to itself. So, Lord, if You do not heal our nature with Your grace and do not infuse in us the power of Your charity through the Holy Spirit, we shall not be able to love You with the supernatural love with which You deserve to be loved. And since You command us, Lord, to love You with a love such as this, and yet we cannot do it without Your help, give us Your grace so that we can fulfill this sweet office. Grant that we may love You, if not as much as You deserve (for no one can do this but Yourself), at least to love You as much as we can, with all our heart and strength.

Grant that we may love You with a simple and disinterested love and love nothing else more than You, and with a strong love that will refuse no effort or labor for You. Grant that we may love You with an affective and diligent love that will always be occupied with the things of Your service, with a unitive love that will never cease to love You and will never depart from You, and with a prudent love that will never exceed Your laws by misguided zeal or fervor. May we love You with a well-ordered love that will love all things in You and You above all things, and with a pure and chaste love that will love You for Your sake alone. May we love You with a zealous love that will love only Your glory, with a violent love that will tear our hearts from all things earthly and keep them fixed on You until, having passed through the desert of this life, we shall see the splendor of Your beauty and shall love You eternally in the company of the blessed, who never cease to love and praise You, the King of kings.

14

MAN'S GRATITUDE TO GOD

One of the greatest impulses that move the heart to love is the recognition of benefits received. The reason, as the philosophers tell us, is that while good is of itself lovable, everyone is especially inclined to love his own good. Consequently, he who wishes to arouse his heart to the love of God should frequently consider the benefits he has received from God. These benefits are innumerable, but we can reduce them to a certain number for the greater facility of those who wish to practice this pious exercise.

What language and what writings could ever suffice to exhaust the deluge of God's blessings and mercies? Yet, how could we better employ our time and energy than in a consideration of such matters? In order better to understand the grandeur of the divine benefits, let us first consider the excellence of the Giver and our own lowliness, for a gift is the more esteemed and praiseworthy as the giver is more excellent and the recipient is lowlier.

The greatness of the divine Giver is manifested to us in many ways. If you raise your eyes to the heavens, the grandeur and beauty that you see there will tell you of the power of Him who brought forth the heavens merely by His wish and command. Even now, if He so desired, He could create another thousand heavens better than the one He has created and He could do it with greater ease than that with which you open and close your eyes. Or consider the excellence of His knowledge as it is manifested in the marvelous order and harmony of the universe as a whole and in each one of its parts, down to the most insignificant creature. For example, the structure of the body of a bee, a mosquito, or any other insect, however small, would fill you with admiration. The same could be said of the greatness of His goodness, majesty, beauty, mercy, sweetness, benignity, and clemency; they far surpass anything that could be said of them.

Yet this admirable Lord is He who from the heights of the heavens has fixed His gaze upon you, a lowly creature, and in His infinite charity has shown you so many mercies. If you consider who He is and what you are, then even if He were to give you a crumb of bread, He would be deserving of inestimable gratitude by reason of His divine excellence. In this spirit and with these sentiments the holy Job marveled at the generosity of God when he said: "What is a man that You should magnify him? Or why do You set Your heart upon him?" (Job 7:17) The mere fact that God is mindful of man and has a place in His love for a creature so lowly is a source of great wonder for anyone who realizes the greatness of God. What could He do for man that He has not done? And if it is a source of amazement that God should even think of man, how much more amazing it is that He should become man Himself and die on the cross for man's redemption.

Man should therefore consider well the following three points when reflecting upon the benefits he has received: Who bestows the benefits, to whom they are granted, and why they are granted. Who? God. To whom? Man. Why? Out of sheer love. God, who has need of nothing outside Himself and seeks for nothing outside Himself, has loved you from all eternity. He deigned to create you and to bestow innumerable blessings upon you so that He might enable you to share in His glory.

Consider how this great God brought you from non-existence to existence and made you in His image and likeness. Open your eyes to the dignity that is yours. You are not a mere vestige or trace of the Creator, as are other creatures, rather, you are His very image and likeness. Like Him, you are an intellectual being, and like Him, you have free will and knowledge, so that as you now resemble Him in your being and life and operation, you may later become a true likeness of His infinite beauty. And in order that your glory would not be transitory and cease with the passing of time, He made you immortal, so that you could be happy for all eternity. Other creatures have no more than a glimpse of the world and then they disappear. But you have come forth from non-existence to existence, never to return to your former nothingness but always to enjoy eternal life.

Understand your dignity and realize that you have such a capacity for happiness that no other creature could ever fill your desires. God alone can satisfy you. Therefore, seek only God as the spouse of your soul, as the fulfillment of all your desires, and as your ultimate end.

O marvelous dignity of our souls! The King whose beauty causes the sun and moon to pale, whose majesty the heavens and the earth revere, whose wisdom the choirs of angels praise, whose goodness all the blessed in heaven worship, that same King desires to dwell in you as in His palace. Prepare and adorn your temple, daughter of Sion, and receive your King, whose presence will gladden and enrich you. Recall the words of St. Bernard: "Blessed is the soul that each day cleanses her heart to receive her God. Blessed the soul in which the Lord finds rest and a dwelling place, so that it can now say: He who created me dwells in my tabernacle and He will not deny it the peace of heaven, because my soul has prepared for Him a dwelling place and a place of rest on earth."

Look at the magnitude of the love that prompted God to bestow His gifts upon you, whether they be little or great. A father is prompted by no less love in giving his child clothing as when he gives it a rich inheritance, for both the great and the small proceed from the same love. So also, the same infinite love prompts the eternal Father to give to His children the small gifts as well as the great ones. Consequently,

He should be loved in return, no less for the one than for the other. Realize, then, what you owe to God, who created you out of love, even though He knew how poorly you would return His love and how many things you would do contrary to His will. Give thanks to Him for His great benefits and realize that neither in heaven nor on earth will you find anyone who is as truly your father as He is.

Look back at your life and you will begin to understand the countless blessings that you have received from God at every turn. When you were as yet in the womb of your mother, who was it that watched over you? Who made sure that you would not die before you were born? It was the same one who has watched over you even until now, so that you can rightly say with the Psalmist: "From my mother's womb You are my God; depart not from me" (Ps. 21[22]:11). At the time of your birth, who protected you so that you would not be numbered among those infants that seem to have been born to die rather than to live? And since the day of your birth, how many dangers, diseases, and sudden misfortunes has the Lord in His merciful providence spared you, holding back the evils and harm that could have befallen you and of which you were not even aware?

I beg you not to dismiss this great blessing, for it is deserving of singular gratitude to God. What infirmity or wound does one man suffer that another man could not suffer equally as well? As descendants of Adam, we are all children of the same father. We are all conceived in original sin and we have all committed personal sins. Why is one man lame, another deaf, and another blind? Why do certain ones suffer from cancer, tuberculosis, or some other disease? Why does this or that person pass day and night in continual pain, knowing scarcely an hour of happiness or relief? Yet the Lord has exempted you from all such sickness and suffering so that you are master of your own body and can enjoy many peaceful hours. How much you owe to God for such a singular blessing! You are a sinner like the rest of men and equally deserving of affliction like the others, but God has spared you while others endure pain and suffering.

You also cannot overlook the daily care that the Lord has for you. Consider how difficult it is for some men to provide for their daily sustenance. Some earn their daily bread by the sweat of their brow, and some, in the midst of great dangers to their soul. Others do so with constant effort and affliction to their spirit, and others, in peril of their life. Even at the cost of great efforts and dangers, some men are scarcely able to earn enough for their daily bread. But you, perhaps, each day find the table set and well provided with food and all that is necessary for your daily life.

If you consider the creatures of this world, you will see that they have been made for your service and welfare. They are part of the heritage that your heavenly Father has left to you. How great, then, must be the divine goodness that has provided so many things for you who do not merit them, even after your many sins and faults whereby you deserve to lose them. How many times have you been frivolously playing or swearing or committing some sin at the very moment that He was bestowing His gifts upon you? And how many times have you used these very gifts in a sinful manner?

The creatures of this world are the servants through which God provides for your nourishment. So, do not be so childish that you are unmindful of the Father who brought you forth while you give all your love to the servants that care for you, for they would not serve you unless they had been commanded to do so. Abandon the things of this world in order to follow your true Father.

The very benefits that God has bestowed on other

creatures have been given for man's benefit, and not for the creatures themselves. This is one of the most consoling truths in the created universe. The beauty and power of the sun, the moon, and the stars, and the beauty of trees and flowers and precious stones, to whom do they give more profit or delight than to man? The perfume and color and beauty of the rose, to whom are they more pleasing than to man? If you can appreciate this truth, then you will realize that all the beauties and perfections of creatures are for your benefit, because all of them were made for you. See, then, how much more you owe to God than you realize, because all the good that He has bestowed on creatures He has thereby bestowed also on you.

What a great spectacle is this visible world if you realize that all the creatures in it are gifts sent to you from God. Even more, they are messages addressed to you from the Creator. Here God is; here He speaks to you; here He teaches you and seeks to draw you to Himself. How is it, then, that in the midst of all these marvels and signs of His goodness, you do not know Him? How is it that in spite of such great benefits you do not love Him? Why is it that your heart never asks: "Who is this that has bestowed so many mercies on me? Who is this that in so many ways reveals Himself to me? Who is this that in so many different ways seeks to draw me to His love? Who is this that by so many testimonies and proofs seeks to make me know Him? Who is this that so loves me that He created all things for my service and benefit? Who is this that out of pure goodness and without any merits on my part, desired to be my Good Shepherd, the Lord of my house, the defender of my goods, the healer of my sickness and wounds, and the provider for all my wants?"

Why is it that in spite of so many blessings, God is not loved? Why, in spite of so many signs and testimonies, does He remain hidden from us? He offers Himself to us through so many of His creatures, but we do not find Him. He works so many wonders for us, but we do not know Him. Such is the effect of sin's corruption that it makes us blind to His splendor and insensible to His love.

Not only the obligations of justice but our very needs and poverty urge us to be mindful of the Creator if we wish to attain happiness and perfection. We know well that creatures are not generally born with their full perfection. The same cause that gave them their beginning and origin must also bestow on them their completion and perfection. Then realize, rational creature, that this is also your condition. You are not yet fully made and perfect, but much is lacking to your perfection. This should be evident to you from the constant longings of your very being, which feels the need for something more and yearns for greater perfection. God desired that you should hunger still and that your needs should bring you to Him. It is not because of His poverty and want that He did not perfect you at the beginning, but because of His love. Not that you should be poor, but that you should be humble; not that you should be needy, but that He would always have you near Him.

If, therefore, you are poor, needy, blind, why do you not go to the Father who made you, so that He can supply what is wanting to you? David did this very thing: "Your hands have made me and formed me. Give me understanding and I will learn Your commandments" (Psalm 118 [119]:73). It is as if David had said: "Your hands, Lord, have fashioned all that I have and whatever is in me, but the work is not yet completed. From whom shall I seek that which is lacking to me, except from Him who has given me all that I possess? Grant me light, Lord; illumine the eyes of one blind from birth so that he may know You and may thus see completed what You have begun in him."

God alone can create without defects, augment without confusion, enrich without ostentation, and give complete satisfaction without the possession of many things. Possessing God, man is poor and content, rich and naked, alone and happy, dispossessed of everything but master of all things. With good reason does the wise man say: "One is as it were rich, when he hath nothing, and another is as it were poor, when he hath great riches" (Proverbs 13:7). Wealthy indeed is the pauper who possesses God, as did St. Francis of Assisi. Poor indeed is the rich man who lacks God, as do many of the lords of the world. Of what avail are all the power and wealth of many riches if, with all that, you live a life beset with cares and torn with desires that you cannot fulfill, in spite of all your possessions? Of what value are gorgeous clothes and delicate fare if these things cannot appease the anxiety and longing of your heart and soul? During the night there are many restless turnings on the soft and comfortable bed of the rich man and they cannot be cured by a well-filled purse.

15

CREATION OF THE ANGELS

Infinitely happy and glorious in the vision of His own divine beauty, God is also magnificent and generous. Since He is supremely good and diffusive of His goodness, He was not content to communicate His blessings merely to the creatures of this visible world. He likewise willed to create higher creatures to whom He could communicate the riches of His happiness and glory. It was as if God did not wish to be alone in His happiness and for that reason, He created two excellent types of creatures in His own image and likeness that would be capable of receiving a share in His glory. Thus, God created the angels in heaven and men on earth. The angels are purely spiritual substances, while men are spiritual substances united to bodies.

But the works of God are perfect, as He Himself is, and since He had created these two kinds of creatures for so noble an end, He also provided them with the powers and perfections necessary for attaining that end. Shabby and tattered men are not admitted to the palaces of kings, but only those who are neat and properly dressed. So also, sensual and carnal men cannot enter into the heavenly mansion of the King of kings, for they are spiritually shabby and tattered. Under one condition will the Lord grant admission to the kingdom of heaven: that men be faithful and obedient to Him and use well the graces and benefits received from Him. Then they can hope to obtain their sovereign good. But if they act otherwise, they will lose all because of their sin.

This same condition was placed upon all the angels after their creation. They were to enter into the divine presence and worship at the throne of God only after they had given proof of their obedience and submission to Him and had resolved to use their blessings and graces for His honor and glory. One group of angels, recognizing that all the goods and gifts they possessed were from God, gave thanks to Him, humbled themselves before Him, and with all their love offered to be His faithful servants forever and to obey His laws. These good angels were then confirmed in grace and raised to the beatific vision of the divine beauty and they shall possess it for all eternity.

Among the angels there was one who was especially perfect and beautiful and, according to St. Gregory, he was the most excellent of all the angels. Consequently, he should have been most grateful, most humble, and most obedient to the Creator who had so wonderfully exalted him. But he was not. Rather, enamored of his own beauty, he became puffed up with pride and sought by his own power to be like unto God. As a punishment for his ingratitude and pride, he was cast out of that glorious place where only the humble dwell. Likewise cast out was a multitude of angels who had followed Lucifer's example and counsel.

The evil angels were obstinate in their malice and since they despaired of ever returning to the position that they had forfeited by their pride, they cultivated a fierce hatred for the God who had condemned them to hell. As a result of their hatred, they work with all their skill and knowledge to lessen His glory and to lead men from His service. Unable to earn a place in heaven, they strive to gain power on earth by deceiving miserable men. Thus, ignorant men are led to the worship of devils and idols, malicious men are gradually weakened until they become apostates from the true Church, and hundreds of new sects and religions are introduced into the world for the promulgation of false beliefs.

Not content with attacking and weakening the faith of men, the devils often persuade and convince them that the human soul is mortal and that there is nothing to life but birth and death. Once they have achieved this, they lead these wretched men into all manner of vices and baseness, as is evident in any nation that disregards God or denies His existence. Such men live like animals, for they

seek nothing but the present and are interested only in those things that pertain to the body. This is the degeneracy to which men can fall when they heed the instigations of the devil, the father of lies, and forget completely that they have been made in the image and likeness of God and are capable of possessing Him for all eternity.

16

GOD'S CARE FOR ALL HIS CREATURES

We shall close our meditations with the general care and providence that God shows for all His creatures. At the outset we should note that there are two kinds of efficient cause: the one is sufficient to produce something, but once the effect has been produced, it exerts no more influence, as in the case of the architect who makes a house or the painter who paints a picture. The other not only produces the thing, but also preserves it in being after it has been made, as we see in the rays of light caused by the sun, for if the sun should become dark or cease to exist, the rays of light would also disappear.

Catholic faith teaches that the sovereign Lord is the

cause of all created things because He gave them their existence and that He also preserves them in the being that He gave them. So great is the dependence of creatures on the Creator that if He were for a moment to turn away from them, they would immediately be annihilated and sink back into the nothingness from which they came.

God must be present in some way to all things that exist, sustaining them not only by His presence and power, but by His very essence. To understand this, we should observe that all other causes produce their effects by virtue of the power they possess, as fire causes heat in other things by reason of the heat it possesses. Nevertheless, in God there is no distinction between His power and His essence, for in His lofty and exalted nature there are no accidents or properties in the strict sense of the word. Everything in God is God, without any admixture or composition. Moreover, wherever there is any part of God, it is all God, because His supreme simplicity does not permit any division whereby part of Him could be in one place and part in another. Lastly, cause and effect must in some way be united and be in contact with each other, and since being is the most universal and most intimate effect in created things, it follows that God is present in the most intimate part of all things. For that reason, God is said to fill the heavens and the earth. He is entire in all the world and entire in each part of the world.

But God not only preserves the being of all creatures, He is also the cause of all their movements and activities. Thus, no created thing can move a hand or foot or open its mouth or open and close its eyes save by the power of God. He is, in a sense, more the cause of the movement than is the creature that moves. Avicenna, an Arabian philosopher, taught that God does no more than assist in the order and movement of the heavens and that by means of the heavenly movements He governs all other things in the lower world. But Christian philosophy goes even further and teaches that the First Cause, which is God, cooperates in the movement and activity of all lower causes. Consequently, all the effects of these lower causes can be attributed more truly to the First Cause who made them than to those that immediately produce the effects. Similarly, it is more proper to say that the painter paints the picture rather than the brush with which he works.

If we consider our relationship with God from the aspect of our dependence on Him, we shall find that there are three ways in which some things can depend on others. Some depend on others for their creation or production, but after receiving existence, they no longer need an extrinsic cause for conservation in being, as is the case of a painting or any other artificial thing that comes from the hand of the artist. Other things depend on their causes in the same way that the life of the body depends on the presence and power of the soul, whereby it lives and continues in existence. Thirdly, some things depend on their causes for the perfection or fullness of their being, as does the student on the professor who teaches him or the wife on the husband from whom she receives the necessities of life.

These three types of dependence create a close bond among the things that are interrelated and are at the same time the motive of great love. As a result, all effects have a natural love for the causes that produce them, sustain them, or from which they seek their full perfection. From the first kind of dependence, we see the great love that children have for their parents and parents for their children. By reason of the second type of dependence, it is natural for the other members of the body to protect the head, which is one of the most vital members of the human body. And by reason of the third type of dependence, we see the great love that a wife has for her husband, for she receives from him many things that contribute to her perfection.

The same three kinds of dependence are to be found in our relationship with God, and in an eminent degree. Since He has given us existence, He ought to be loved by us as a father is loved by his children. Since He conserves us in being, He should be loved as the head is loved by the members. Then, since He offers us the plenitude of perfection, he should be loved as the bridegroom is loved by the bride. Acknowledge these obligations and, knowing what you have been and what you are and what you hope to be, love Him who has done so much for you and will continue to do so much for you.

Grant that I may love You, Lord, for I am Your creature and You are my Maker, from whom I have received my very being and existence. Let the waters run back to their source, let the effect return to the cause that produced it,

and let the creature turn back to the Creator who fashioned it.

Do not let me be guilty of such treason, Lord, that I would surrender the keys of Your mansion to anyone but You. I am Yours, Lord, I shall remain Yours, and Yours I desire to be forever. Receive me as Your own and do not reject that which You have made for Yourself.

On whom shall I fix my eyes, Lord, and whom shall I love but You? For Your hands have created me, Your providence sustains me, and Your creatures serve me. Through whose power do I exist and from whom do I have all that I possess, if not from You? You alone are the source of all my good and the storehouse of all my treasures.

You planted me by Your hand when You created me and since now You conserve me in being by the care and watering of Your divine providence, who but You shall harvest the fruit of this land? I am Your acreage and soil and You are my Lord and Master. All the plants of this land—my faculties and powers—are for Your service. For You are the flowers of my desires and the fruits of my good works. May my eyes bless You, my tongue praise You, my hands serve You, my feet walk along the path of Your commandments, and my heart be inflamed with Your love. May my memory never forget You, my intellect ever contemplate You, and my will delight only in You. Let such be the harvest and fruits of this land. Surround it, Lord, with a wall of fire and close all its gates so that none but You can enter in. I adjure and command you, all created things, that you touch nothing in this land of His. Let all be Yours, Lord, and let all be used in Your service. Let all other creatures die to this love and let me die to them.

May I love You, Lord, for You alone can finish the work You have begun in me. You alone can give my soul its full perfection. May I love You, Lord, with an intimate and fervent love. May I have the arms of good desires and good affections with which to embrace You, sweet Spouse of my soul, from whom I hope for all good.

The ivy embraces the tree in so many parts that the whole vine seems to be made up of arms whereby it can be more firmly attached to the tree and can climb upward until it reaches its full perfection. You are the tree, Lord, that I desire to embrace and cling to, so that I may attain that which is still lacking to me. Let my soul grow like the ivy in virtues and graces when it embraces You. Let me be all arms so that I may embrace You in every part.

Help me, Lord, and lead me far along Your path, for the weight of my mortality impedes my progress. You, Lord and Savior, who ascended to the height of the Cross in order to draw all things to Yourself, You who in Your great love united two natures in one Person to become one with us, stoop to unite our hearts with You in such a strong bond of love that they will become one with You.

In Your hands, Lord, are all my days, past and present and future. In the past I received from You the being that I now have. In the present You preserve me in life, as the sun does the rays of light that emanate from it. In the future my final perfection and the fulfillment of all my desires must come from Your hand, when my soul will find perfect rest and be united with You to share in the happiness for which You created me.

Look down upon me, Lord, with Your merciful and paternal gaze and infuse into my soul the rays of Your mercy and love so that, raising my eyes to You in humility and reverence, I may receive the blessing of Your light. Looking to You, I repeat with the Psalmist: "My eyes are ever toward the Lord, for He shall pluck my feet out of the snare. Look You upon me and have mercy on me, for I am alone and poor" (Psalm 24[25]:15-16).

In the same spirit let us all say: "To You have I lifted

up my eyes, who dwell in heaven. Behold, as the eyes of servants are on the hands of their masters, as the eyes of the handmaid are on the hands of her mistress, so are our eyes unto the Lord our God, until He have mercy on us" (Psalm 122[123]:1-2)